the new cook

acknowledgments

With thanks to Matt Handbury and Jackie Frank, for such a brilliant opportunity; to Jane Roarty, for her inspiration and most passionate support; to Sara Beaney, a brilliant designer, for making my book beautiful; to Michèle, for all the weekends and late nights of toil; to Rowena, my editor, who kept me motivated; to Catie, Anne, Anna, Mark and all of the rest of the Murdoch Books team, for your patience and for such a great opportunity; to Mum and Dad, for the endless stream of support and understanding – I guess I'll always be a running-late sort of person – thanks for waiting; to my friends William and Sibella, who tasted and tested, and supported me through the book; to my partner and friend Billy – words can't describe – thanks; to Jody, my inspiration, colleague, friend, and strength, who enabled me to get this far – thank you; to the Antico family, for searching the markets for the most amazing fresh fruit and vegetables, and for entertaining me when I come to the shop; to Con and James of Demcos Seafood Providores, for the freshest, sweetest seafood; to Petrina, who stuck with the cracking pace, for the long and sometimes painful task of photography, thank you for your input and energy in making this book a visual feast.

Recipes and Styling: Donna Hay
Photographer: Petrina Tinslay
Art Director/Designer: Sara Beaney
Designer: Michèle Lichtenberger
Editor: Rowena Lennox
Additional Photography: William Meppem, front cover, p.37, p.84 right, p.107 top right, p.136; Quentin Bacon p.125, p.182.
White bowls, plates and accessories: Pillivuyt from Hale Imports, telephone (02) 9938 2400

HarperCollins books may be purchased for educational, business, or sales promotional use. For information please write: Special Markets Department, HarperCollins Publishers Inc., 10 East 53rd Street, New York, NY 10022.

Originally published in Australia in 1997 by Murdoch Books® , a division of Murdoch Magazines Pty Ltd.

FIRST U.S. EDITION PUBLISHED 2003

Library of Congress Cataloging-in-Publication Data has been applied for

ISBN 0-06-056632-9

03 04 05 06 07/10 9 8 7 6 5 4 3 2 1

the new cook

donna hay

WILLIAM MORROW
An Imprint of HarperCollins*Publishers*

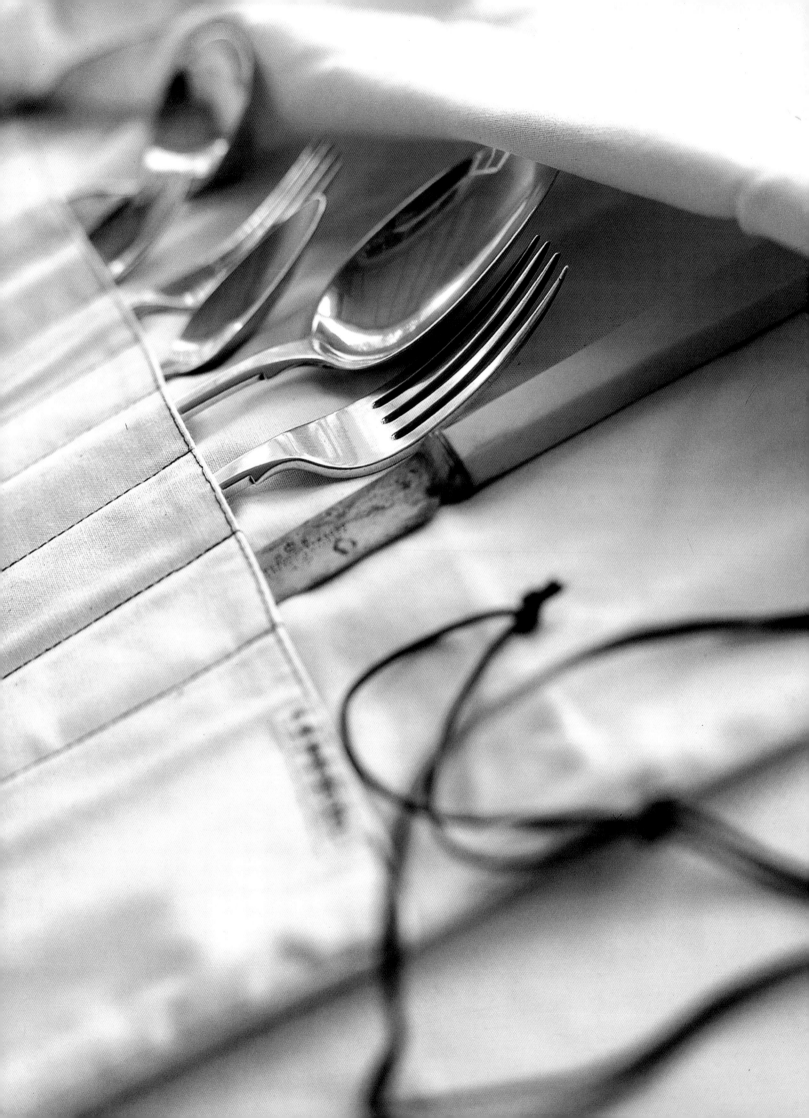

introduction

I believe that what makes good food is a combination of fresh ingredients and uncomplicated layers of flavour. When you start with quality produce, a few simple flavours will complement and contrast with your base ingredients to create the perfect taste experience. Think of food with passion, not anxiety, and feel free to substitute and add ingredients as you please. This is often how personalised culinary masterpieces are created. More information about ingredients marked with an asterisk* can be found in the glossary (page 182). *The new cook* is a guide to quick preparation, easy cooking techniques and inventive serving ideas. Use it to go step-by-step through the basics and on to a feast of easy-to-follow recipes that will make preparing food a simple but satisfying part of your everyday life. Cooking is my passion. I hope that *the new cook* will help to make it yours.

eggs

basics

Eggs can be the most simple and the most difficult of foods to cook. When you understand a few basic properties of the humble egg, the mystery of cooking one to perfection will be revealed.

selection and storage

I prefer true free-range eggs for their flavour, and for their bright yolks and thick whites. There are a few good reasons for storing eggs in their carton in the fridge. Egg shells are porous and they will absorb any strong food smells in your fridge. Eggs are packed with the pointed end down so the yolk stays centred and the air sac at the blunt end has less pressure on it and is not damaged. Storage life depends on the freshness of the eggs when purchased. Around 2½–3 weeks is an egg's maximum fridge life.

boiling

For eggs at room temperature slipped into boiling water:
SOFT BOILED
2–3 minutes
FIRM WHITE, SOFT YOLK
5–6 minutes
HARD BOILED
10 minutes
To centre the yolk, add the egg to water that has been stirred to create a whirlpool and continue stirring for 1 minute while cooking.

freshness

Freshness can be tested in two ways:
1 When it's cracked onto a plate, the yolk of a fresh egg will sit high and look plump and rounded. The fresh white should be thick and a little cloudy, and cling to the yolk.
2 Drop an egg into a bowl of water. If the egg floats on its side, it is fresh; if it floats vertically with the rounded end up, it is 2–3 weeks old. An egg that floats on the surface of the water has seen better days and is ready for the garbage. The larger the air pocket in the egg, the older it is.

poaching

I'm a self-confessed bad egg-poacher but I'm still trying! Have a 7–10cm (3–4 inch) frying pan full of rapidly simmering water. Break each egg into a cup and gently slip the egg into the pan. Stir the rapidly simmering water to form a whirlpool for a neat oval-shaped poached egg. Allow the egg to cook for 3–4 minutes before removing it from the pan with a slotted spoon. To test for readiness, press the egg with your finger. The white should be firm and the yolk should be soft.

tips for success

It is sometimes better to use eggs at room temperature, especially when beating whole eggs or egg whites, or using them as an emulsifier. Eggs are extremely sensitive to heat and there may be only a minute between a tender, moist egg and a tough, dry, rubbery egg. When adding eggs to anything hot (such as soups), add a little of the hot substance to the eggs first. Salt relaxes the protein in eggs, making them easier to blend. However, if salt is added to eggs that are to be scrambled, poached or made into an omelette, the eggs will become thin and may break up when cooked.

scrambling

Start by melting a tablespoon of butter in a frying pan over medium heat. Place 2 eggs in a bowl and whisk with 1–2 tablespoons of milk or cream. Pour eggs and milk into frying pan and slowly stir with a wooden spoon. Stir just enough to break up the eggs but don't overstir so the eggs become a lumpy mass. Scrambled eggs should be soft and creamy with firm pieces of egg throughout. If overcooked, scrambled eggs will weep liquid because of the tightening of the proteins in the egg.
Add anything you like to scrambled eggs. Additions such as fresh herbs, smoked salmon, aged cheddar cheese, caviar, salmon roe, sour cream, blue cheese, truffle slices and seasonings should be stirred through just before serving.

frying

Heat 2 teaspoons of oil in a small frying pan over medium heat. Break the egg shell and gently slip the egg into the pan. Cook for 1–2 minutes or until the egg is cooked to your liking.

duck egg

free-range hen egg

quail egg

soft-boiled egg

essential with eggs – hot buttered toast

poached egg

scrambled eggs

STEP ONE
Place the butter and oil in a 23cm (9 inch) non-stick frying pan over low heat and cook until the butter has melted. Add the onions to the pan.

caramelised onion frittata

1 tablespoon butter
1 tablespoon oil
3 onions, sliced
8 eggs
¾ cup (6 fl oz) cream (pouring or single) or milk
cracked black pepper
½ cup grated aged cheddar cheese
1 tablespoon thyme leaves

variations

PUMPKIN FRITTATA
Add ½ cup mashed pumpkin or orange sweet potato (kumara) when whisking the eggs.

BLUE CHEESE AND POTATO FRITTATA
When the onions have cooked in the pan, sprinkle 1 cup cooked cubed potato over them. Pour in the egg mixture and sprinkle blue cheese instead of cheddar over eggs.

ANTIPASTO FRITTATA
After adding the eggs to the pan, top them with char-grilled (broiled) antipasto vegetables such as capsicum (red or green bell pepper), eggplant (aubergine) and zucchini (courgette). Sprinkle the frittata with the cheese and complete steps three and four.

STEP TWO
Cook the onions, stirring occasionally, for 10–15 minutes or until golden brown, soft and caramelised.

STEP THREE
Place the eggs, cream and pepper in a bowl and whisk to combine. Pour the egg mixture over the onions in the frying pan and sprinkle with the cheese and thyme. Cook the frittata for 5–6 minutes or until almost set.

STEP FOUR
To finish cooking, place the frittata under a preheated hot grill for 1 minute. Cut into wedges and serve on hot buttered toast or with a spicy chutney. Serves 4 to 6.

caramelised onion frittata

asparagus and poached eggs with brown butter   bacon and egg pie

roast pumpkin and soft quail egg salad

angel food cake

asparagus and poached eggs with brown butter

85g (2¾ oz) butter
1 tablespoon sage leaves
500g (1 lb) fresh asparagus
4 eggs
shaved parmesan cheese
cracked black pepper

Place the butter and sage in a saucepan over low heat, allow to bubble until golden brown. Keep warm.
Trim the ends from the asparagus and steam until tender. While the asparagus is steaming fill a frying pan with water and bring to a simmer.
Place the eggs in the simmering water one at a time and poach for 3–4 minutes or until the whites are firm and the yolks are soft (see page 10).
Place the asparagus on warmed serving plates. Remove the eggs from the pan with a slotted spoon and place on top of the asparagus. Top with the brown butter, parmesan shavings and lots of cracked pepper. Serve immediately. Serves 4.

bacon and egg pie

1 quantity or 250g (8 oz) shortcrust pastry*
filling
6 eggs
1 cup (8 fl oz) milk
4 rashers bacon, chopped
⅓ cup grated aged cheddar cheese
2 tablespoons chopped chives
1 tablespoon chopped dill
2 teaspoons Dijon mustard
cracked black pepper
6 thin rashers bacon, extra, rind removed

Roll out the pastry on a lightly floured surface until 3mm (⅛ inch) thick. Place in a 25cm (10 inch) pie dish and trim the edges. Refrigerate for 30 minutes. Prick the base of the pastry and line with non-stick baking paper. Fill the shell with baking weights or rice and bake at 180°C (350°F) for 5 minutes. Remove the weights and paper, and cook for a further 5 minutes. (This process keeps the pastry crisp when adding wet ingredients to the pastry shell.)
Place the eggs and milk in a bowl and whisk to combine. Add the bacon, cheese, chives, dill, mustard and pepper and mix to combine. Pour the mixture into the pastry shell, top with the extra bacon rashers and bake at 160°C (315°F) for 35–45 minutes or until the pie is set. Serve in hot or cold wedges with a rocket (arugula) salad. Serves 6.

roast pumpkin and soft quail egg salad

500g (1 lb) jap* or sweet pumpkin, sliced
olive oil
cracked black pepper
½ cup marinated olives
200g (6½ oz) marinated fetta cheese
3 tablespoons oregano leaves
150g (5 oz) baby rocket (arugula)
8 soft-boiled quail eggs
balsamic vinegar

Place the pumpkin in a baking dish and drizzle with olive oil and season with pepper. Bake at 180°C (350°F) for 35 minutes or until golden and soft. Allow to cool.
Toss the olives, fetta, oregano and rocket in a bowl. Place the salad on serving plates with the pumpkin, top each with two quail eggs and dress with a splash of balsamic vinegar and olive oil. Serves 4.

angel food cake

1 cup plain (all-purpose) flour
1½ cups sugar
12 egg whites
½ teaspoon cream of tartar
2 teaspoons grated lemon rind
½ teaspoon vanilla extract
berries to serve

Sift the flour and half the sugar into a bowl and set aside. Place the egg whites and cream of tartar in a bowl and beat until soft peaks form. Gradually add the remaining sugar to the egg whites and beat until thick and glossy. Fold the lemon rind, vanilla and flour mixture into the egg whites. Pour the mixture into an ungreased 23cm (9 inch) angel food cake tin and bake at 190°C (375°F) for 30 minutes or until the cake is cooked when tested with a skewer. Invert the tin and allow the cake to cool. Run a knife around the edge of the tin to release the cake. Serve with mixed berries. Dust with icing (confectioner's) sugar if desired. Serves 8.

pasta

basics

cooking fresh pasta

Fresh pasta needs less water than dried pasta. To cook fresh pasta, have a large saucepan of rapidly boiling salted water ready. Make sure you have enough boiling water for the pasta to cook in. Add a little oil to the water, so the pasta doesn't stick together. Add the pasta to the pan, ensure the water stays boiling, and stir slowly for 10 seconds to separate the pasta. Boil pasta for 2–4 minutes (the time depends on the type of pasta you are using) or until it is al dente.

cooking dried pasta

The most common mistake people make when cooking dried pasta is not having enough boiling water. Have a large saucepan of rapidly boiling salted water ready. Add a little oil and the pasta to the pan, and stir for 20 seconds to separate the pasta. Boil for 10–14 minutes. (Cooking time varies depending on the shape of pasta as well as the type of the flours used in the pasta.) Cook the pasta until it is al dente.

al dente

Al dente means 'to the tooth'. When it's cooked, pasta should be soft but still firm when you bite into it. The easiest way to tell whether pasta is al dente is to remove a piece from the saucepan and test it between your teeth. The pasta should have some texture when you bite into it, but it should not be dry and hard in the middle.

drying fresh pasta

To dry fresh pasta, hang it over a suspended wooden spoon or a clean broom handle in a dry, airy place for 1–2 hours (the time depends on the weather). Leave it hanging until it's dry and hard. Store the pasta in airtight containers. Alternatively, fresh pasta can be frozen in airtight plastic bags or containers for up to 6 months. See glossary (page 186) for a recipe for fresh pasta.

draining cooked pasta

To drain cooked pasta, pour it into a colander and shake the colander to remove excess water. If you are serving it hot, use pasta immediately and do not rinse it. If you are serving it cold, rinse pasta under warm and then cold water. You can also refrigerate pasta and use it within 3 days.

herb fettuccine

chilli linguine

pasta machine

cracked pepper linguine

drying pappardelle

boiling pasta

chilli pasta with prawns and lime

pasta with roast sweet potato and fetta

roast vegetable lasagne

chilli pasta with prawns and lime

750g (1½ lb) medium green (raw) prawns (shrimp), peeled
1 tablespoon olive oil
2 teaspoons cracked pepper
1 tablespoon chopped coriander (cilantro)
400g (14 oz) chilli-flavoured pasta
250g (8 oz) fresh asparagus, trimmed
4 limes, halved
125g (4 oz) baby English spinach leaves
¼ cup basil leaves
olive oil to serve
cracked black pepper

Place the prawns, oil, pepper and coriander in a bowl and toss to combine. Place the pasta in a saucepan of boiling salted water and cook until al dente.
Drain the pasta and keep warm. Boil or steam the asparagus until tender. Chop into 5cm (2 inch) pieces. Place the prawns and limes on a hot char grill (broiler) or barbecue and cook for 1 minute on each side or until tender. Toss the prawns with the pasta, asparagus, spinach and basil.
Squeeze the juice from the grilled limes over the pasta and top with a drizzle of olive oil and some cracked black pepper. Serve immediately. Serves 4.

pasta with roast sweet potato and fetta

750g (1½ lb) orange sweet potato (kumara)
1 tablespoon oil
salt
1 tablespoon oil, extra
3 leeks, chopped
1 tablespoon fresh rosemary
400g (14 oz) pasta of your choice
2 tablespoons butter
185g (6 oz) marinated fetta cheese, chopped
250g (8 oz) baby English spinach leaves
cracked black pepper
grated pecorino or parmesan cheese

Peel and chop the sweet potato and place in a baking dish with the oil and salt. Bake at 200ºC (400ºF) for 30 minutes or until soft and brown.
Place the extra oil in a frying pan over medium heat. Add the leeks and rosemary and cook for 7 minutes or until golden and soft.
Place the pasta in a saucepan of boiling salted water and cook until al dente. Drain and place in a large warmed bowl. Add the sweet potato, leek mixture, butter and fetta. Toss to combine.
Place piles of spinach on warmed serving plates and top with the pasta, pepper and pecorino. Serves 4.

roast vegetable lasagne

2 eggplants (aubergines), sliced
salt
olive oil
250g (8 oz) English spinach leaves
3 large sheets fresh pasta, lightly cooked
12 roma tomatoes,* sliced
1 cup basil leaves
1 cup oregano leaves
1 cup shaved parmesan cheese
1 cup grated mozzarella cheese
extra oregano leaves

Place the eggplant in a colander and sprinkle with salt. Allow to drain for 30 minutes. Rinse and pat dry. Brush the slices with olive oil. Pan fry or char grill (broil) until golden on both sides. Set aside. Preheat the oven to 180ºC (350ºF). Place the spinach in boiling water for 10 seconds to blanch, then drain well.
Line the base of an 18 x 28cm (7 x 11 inch) baking tray with non-stick baking paper. Place a layer of pasta in the baking tray and top with slices of tomato, basil, oregano, eggplant and spinach. Sprinkle with parmesan and mozzarella. Repeat the layers and top the cheese with the extra oregano leaves. Bake for 40 minutes or until cooked through. Serves 6.

pasta with roast tomato sauce

24 roma tomatoes,* halved
6 cloves garlic
2 tablespoons olive oil
1 tablespoon oregano leaves
2 teaspoons olive oil, extra
2 onions, chopped
1 tablespoon basil leaves
400g (14 oz) pasta of your choice
cracked black pepper
shaved parmesan cheese

Place the tomatoes, garlic, oil and oregano in a baking dish and toss to combine. Bake at 160ºC (315ºF) for 45 minutes or until the tomatoes are soft.
Place the tomato mixture in a food processor and process until finely chopped. Heat the extra oil in a saucepan over medium heat and add the onions. Cook for 5 minutes or until golden. Add the tomato mixture and basil and cook for 5 minutes or until heated through.
Cook the pasta in a saucepan of rapidly boiling salted water until al dente. Drain. Place in a serving dish and top with the tomato sauce. Top with pepper and parmesan. Serves 4.

pasta with roast tomato sauce

angel hair pasta with tuna

400g (14 oz) angel hair pasta*
120g (4 oz) rocket (arugula), roughly chopped
350g (11¼ oz) sashimi tuna,* thinly sliced
½ cup shaved parmesan cheese
2–3 tablespoons chilli oil*
cracked black pepper
lime wedges

Place the pasta in a large saucepan of boiling salted water and cook until al dente. Drain. While still hot, toss the pasta with the rocket, tuna, parmesan, chilli oil and pepper. To serve, pile the pasta on plates and top with a squeeze of lime juice. Serves 4.

pasta with greens

400g (14 oz) pappardelle or wide fettuccine
1 tablespoon olive or basil oil*
2 cloves garlic, crushed
85g (2¾ oz) baby English spinach leaves
85g (2¾ oz) baby beetroot 'beet' tops
85g (2¾ oz) rocket (arugula)
185g (6 oz) firm goat's cheese, crumbled
cracked black pepper
baby salted capers (rinsed and dried)

Place the pasta in a saucepan of rapidly boiling salted water and cook until al dente. Drain and keep warm. Heat the oil in a saucepan over medium heat. Add the garlic and cook until golden. Remove from the heat. Place the greens in a bowl and toss through the hot oil. Place the pasta in serving bowls and top with the greens, goat's cheese, pepper and capers. Serves 4.

pasta with baby leeks

2 tablespoons olive oil
8 baby leeks, trimmed
3 tablespoons marjoram leaves
1 tablespoon thyme leaves
400g (14 oz) herb fettuccine
2 large ripe tomatoes, sliced
200g (6½ oz) smoked mozzarella cheese, sliced
cracked black pepper

Heat the oil in a frying pan over low heat. Add the leeks, marjoram and thyme. Cook for 8 minutes or until the leeks are golden and soft.
Place the pasta in a saucepan of boiling salted water and cook until al dente. Pile the pasta onto serving plates and top with the leek mixture, tomatoes, mozzarella and pepper. Place under a hot grill (broiler) for 1 minute or until the cheese is melted and golden. Serves 4.

spaghetti with grilled chicken and asparagus

400g (14 oz) spaghetti
3 chicken breast fillets
olive oil
300g (10 oz) fresh asparagus
2 red capsicums (bell peppers), quartered
dressing
3 tablespoons lemon juice
1 tablespoon seeded mustard
2 tablespoons olive oil
1 tablespoon dill leaves

Place the spaghetti in a saucepan of rapidly boiling salted water and cook until al dente. Drain and keep warm. Brush the chicken breasts with a little oil and place on a hot char grill (broiler) or barbecue, or in a frying pan. Cook for 2–3 minutes each side or until cooked through. Blanch* the asparagus in boiling water until bright green. Brush the capsicums and asparagus with oil and place on the grill with the chicken. Cook for a further 2 minutes.
To serve, place the spaghetti in bowls. Slice the chicken and capsicums and place on top with the asparagus. Combine the dressing ingredients with a whisk and pour over the pasta. Serve immediately. Serves 4.

pepper linguini with Asian herbs

400g (14 oz) pepper-flavoured linguini
½ cup Thai basil* leaves
¼ cup Vietnamese mint* leaves
2 green chillies, chopped
4 tablespoons salt-reduced soy sauce
2 tablespoons brown sugar
1 tablespoon kaffir lime* juice
2 tablespoons mirin* or sweet white cooking wine
steamed baby bok choy*

Place the linguini in a saucepan of boiling salted water and cook for 3 minutes or until al dente. Drain. Toss the basil and mint through the linguini. Combine the chillies, soy sauce, sugar, lime juice and mirin and pour over the pasta. Toss to combine.
Place on plates and serve with steamed baby bok choy. Serves 4.

angel hair pasta with tuna

pasta with baby leeks

pasta with greens

spaghetti with grilled chicken and asparagus

pepper linguini with Asian herbs

pappardelle with fennel and olives

salmon and wasabi ravioli with kaffir lime sauce

pappardelle with fennel and olives

2 red onions, chopped
2 baby fennel, sliced
2 tablespoons olive oil
3/4 cup (6 fl oz) white wine
375g (12 oz) pappardelle
1/4 cup basil leaves
1 cup olives
10 caper berries or salted capers (rinsed and dried)
6 anchovies, chopped
shaved parmesan cheese
cracked black pepper

Place the onions and fennel in a baking dish and toss with olive oil to coat. Add the wine and bake at 200ºC (400ºF) for 30 minutes or until the fennel is soft.
Place the pappardelle in a large saucepan of boiling salted water and cook until al dente. Drain.
Toss the hot pappardelle with the fennel mixture, basil, olives, caper berries or capers, and anchovies. Serve with parmesan and lots of cracked black pepper. Serves 4.

salmon and wasabi ravioli with kaffir lime sauce

1 quantity or 250g (8 oz) fresh pasta* or 40 wonton wrappers*
filling
300g (10 oz) salmon fillet
1/3 cup crème fraîche or sour cream
125g (4 oz) ricotta cheese
wasabi* to taste (about 1/2 teaspoon)
1 tablespoon chopped dill
cracked pepper
kaffir lime sauce
1 cup (8 fl oz) fish or vegetable stock
6 kaffir lime* leaves, shredded
3/4 cup (6 fl oz) cream

Cut the pasta into 10cm (4 inch) squares and set aside.
To make the filling, cut the salmon into slices 2cm (3/4 inch) thick. Place the salmon, crème fraîche, ricotta, wasabi, dill and pepper in a bowl and mix to combine. Place spoonfuls of the filling on the pasta squares or wonton wrappers and top with another pasta square or wonton wrapper. Press the squares firmly around the edges to seal.
To make the sauce, place the stock, lime leaves and cream in a saucepan and simmer gently until reduced by half.
To cook the ravioli, place in a large saucepan of boiling salted water and cook for 6–8 minutes or until the pasta is al dente. Drain. Place the ravioli in serving bowls and spoon over the sauce. Top with cracked black pepper. Serves 4 as a main or 6 as a starter.

fettuccine with lemon swordfish

400g (14 oz) fettuccine
2 tablespoons olive oil
1 tablespoon grated lemon rind
1 clove garlic, crushed
1 red chilli, chopped
2 tablespoons lemon thyme leaves
2 tablespoons butter
350g (11 1/4 oz) swordfish, cubed
1 lemon, thinly sliced
cracked black pepper
grated parmesan cheese

Place the fettuccine in a saucepan of boiling salted water and cook until al dente. Drain and keep warm.
While the pasta is cooking, heat the oil in a saucepan over medium heat. Add the lemon rind, garlic, chilli and thyme and cook for 3 minutes. Keep warm.
Heat the butter in a frying pan over medium heat. Add the swordfish and cook for 2–3 minutes or until golden and tender.
Remove the swordfish from the pan and keep warm. Add the lemon slices to the pan and cook for 2 minutes each side or until golden.
Toss the swordfish and spice mixture through the fettuccine and place in deep bowls. Top with pepper and parmesan. Serve with the fried lemon slices on the side. Serves 4.

fettuccine with fried basil, garlic and capers

400g (14 oz) fettuccine
3 tablespoons fruity olive oil
1/4 cup basil leaves
5 cloves garlic, crushed
2 tablespoons baby salted capers (rinsed and dried)
2 tablespoons lemon juice
4 bocconcini,* sliced
shaved parmesan cheese
cracked black pepper

Place the fettuccine in a large saucepan of boiling salted water and cook until al dente. Drain and keep warm.
Place the oil in a frying pan over medium heat. Add the basil, garlic and capers and cook until the garlic is golden and the basil is crisp. Add the lemon juice and toss the basil mixture through the pasta.
Place the slices of bocconcini on plates. Top with the pasta and parmesan and a generous sprinkling of cracked black pepper. Serve immediately. Serves 4.

fettuccine with lemon swordfish

fettuccine with fried basil, garlic and capers

rice

basics

It is important to use the appropriate type of rice for a dish or meal, and to cook the rice in the appropriate way. If you want the grains to stick together for ease of eating with chopsticks, for example, don't wash the rice before cooking, and use the absorption method.

varieties or types

short and medium grain

Short- and medium-grain rice have traditionally been used by the English for puddings, although the Japanese use them for everyday sushi, the Spanish for paella and the Chinese eat medium-grain rice at almost every meal. The plump, moist grains stick together when cooked properly, making them easy to eat with chopsticks.

brown

Brown rice comes in long- and short-grain varieties. The outer husk or bran of brown rice is not polished away as it is for white rice. Therefore, brown rice is nutritionally superior to white rice and has a slightly nutty taste. Brown rice takes approximately 40 minutes to cook as the water has to penetrate the bran.

risotto

Sometimes simply labelled risotto rice, the arborio, violone and carnaroli varieties are used to make risotto because the surface starch that is released when the grains are cooked creates a cream in combination with the stock. Carnaroli tends to provide the creamiest result.

long grain

Long-grain rice separates into individual grains when cooked. Jasmine and basmati rice are both long-grain varieties.

wild

Wild rice is not really a rice but the grain from a water grass native to North America. It has a distinctive nutty flavour with a chewy texture and comes with a fairly hefty price tag. You can mix it with other varieties of rice.

glutinous

Glutinous rice comes in plump, opaque grains, which can be either white or black, or short or long. These grains become sticky and sweet when cooked. It is necessary to soak glutinous rice overnight if you are steaming it. It can be used unsoaked if you are cooking it by the absorption method. Predominantly used in sweets, glutinous rice is also the staple rice of some Asian countries.

risotto rice

brown rice

short-grain rice

long-grain, jasmine and basmati rice

white and black glutinous rice

wild rice

basic risotto

4–4½ cups (32–36 fl oz) vegetable
  or chicken stock
1 cup (8 fl oz) dry white wine
1 tablespoon olive oil
1 tablespoon butter

1 onion, finely chopped
2 cups arborio (risotto) rice
½ cup shaved or grated parmesan
  cheese
cracked black pepper

STEP ONE
Place the stock and wine in a saucepan over medium heat and bring to a very slow simmer. Place the olive oil and butter in a heavy-based saucepan over medium heat. Add the onion to the oil and butter. Cook until soft.

STEP TWO
Add the rice to the oil, butter and onion. Cook, stirring, for 1 minute or until the rice is translucent.

STEP THREE
Slowly add 1 cup (8 fl oz) of the stock to the rice and stir constantly until the liquid has been absorbed. Repeat, only adding more stock after the liquid has been absorbed. Continue adding the stock until the rice is soft and the risotto is creamy. If you need more liquid, heat some extra stock or water. The rice grains should be firm but tender.

STEP FOUR
When the rice is almost cooked, stir through the parmesan and pepper. Serve the risotto in deep bowls on a bed of steamed greens and sprinkle generously with cracked black pepper. Serves 4.

basic risotto

sweet potato and chicken risotto

350g (11¼ oz) orange sweet potato (kumara), peeled
  and chopped
4–4½ cups (32–36 fl oz) chicken stock
1 cup (8 fl oz) dry white wine
1 tablespoon olive oil
1 tablespoon butter
2 leeks, chopped
2 chicken breast fillets, chopped
2 cups arborio (risotto) rice
⅓ cup shaved or grated parmesan cheese
2 tablespoons butter, extra
cracked black pepper

Bake the sweet potato in a greased baking dish at 180°C
(350°F) for 25 minutes. Place the stock and wine in a
saucepan and heat to a slow simmer.
Place the oil, butter and leek in a heavy-based saucepan
over medium heat and cook until soft and golden. Add the
chicken and cook for 4 minutes or until browned. Remove
and set aside.
Add the rice to the pan and cook until translucent. Add the
stock a cup at a time and stir continuously (see page 36).
Just before the risotto is cooked, stir through the chicken
mixture and parmesan. Mash half the sweet potato with the
extra butter and add to the risotto.
To serve, place on a serving plate, top with the remaining
sweet potato and add cracked black pepper. Serves 4.

saffron porcini risotto cakes

25g (¾ oz) dry porcini mushrooms*
2 cups (16 fl oz) warm water
¼ teaspoon saffron* threads
¼ cup (2 fl oz) water
2 cups (16 fl oz) vegetable stock
1 cup (8 fl oz) dry white wine
2 tablespoons oil
2 leeks, chopped
2 cups arborio (risotto) rice
1 tablespoon chopped lemon thyme
½ cup grated parmesan cheese
1 teaspoon cracked black pepper
flour to coat
oil for shallow-frying

Soak the porcini mushrooms in warm water for 30 minutes.
Squeeze the water from the porcini and filter through a fine
sieve lined with paper. Set aside. Place the saffron in fresh
water and allow to stand for 5 minutes. Place the porcini
liquid, saffron mixture, stock and wine in a saucepan and
bring to a slow simmer. Place the oil and leeks in a heavy-
based saucepan over medium heat and cook for 5 minutes

or until soft and golden. Add the rice and cook, stirring, until
translucent. Add the stock mixture a cup at a time (see page
36) and stir continuously. When the risotto is almost cooked,
add the chopped porcini, thyme, parmesan and pepper.
Continue cooking until the rice is firm but tender. Allow to
cool for 10 minutes. Shape the risotto into patties and toss in
the flour. Shallow-fry in hot oil. Drain and serve. Serves 6.

miso and shiitake risotto

3 tablespoons miso*
4 cups (32 fl oz) water
½ cup cooking sake* or dry white wine
½ cup cooking sherry
1 teaspoon sesame oil
1 tablespoon peanut oil
2 red chillies, chopped
150g (5 oz) shiitake mushrooms,* sliced
2 cups arborio (risotto) rice
1 tablespoon chopped Vietnamese mint*
2 tablespoons chopped chives
steamed bok choy* to serve
cracked black pepper

Place the miso, water, sake and sherry in a saucepan and
allow to simmer slowly. Place the oils in a heavy-based
saucepan over medium heat. Add the chillies and cook
for 1 minute. Add the mushrooms and cook for 2 minutes
or until soft. Remove the mushrooms and set aside.
Add the rice to the pan and cook, stirring, until translucent.
Add 1 cup (8 fl oz) of the miso liquid at a time (see
page 36) and stir continuously. When the rice is almost
tender, add the mushrooms, mint and chives.
To serve, place the bok choy on plates, top with the risotto
and sprinkle with pepper. Serves 4.

tomato and fennel risotto

6 roma tomatoes*
olive oil
440g (14 oz) can peeled tomatoes, mashed
2 cups (16 fl oz) beef stock
1 cup (8 fl oz) red wine
2 tablespoons olive oil, extra
2 onions, chopped
2 cloves garlic, crushed
3 baby fennel, sliced
2 cups arborio (risotto) rice
⅓ cup grated mature firm goat's cheese
cracked black pepper

Place the roma tomatoes on a baking tray, drizzle with olive
oil and sprinkle over some pepper. Bake at 160°C (315°F)
for 30 minutes. Place the canned tomatoes, stock and wine
in a saucepan and bring to a slow simmer.

sweet potato and chicken risotto

miso and shiitake risotto

saffron porcini risotto cakes

tomato and fennel risotto

Place the extra oil, onions and garlic in a heavy-based saucepan over medium heat and cook for 3 minutes or until soft. Add the fennel and cook for 8–10 minutes. Add the rice and cook, stirring, until translucent. Add the stock mixture a cup at a time, stirring continuously. When the rice is tender but firm, stir in the cheese and pepper. Serve with roasted tomatoes and thinly sliced rare beef. Serves 6.

coconut rice with green chilli

2 cups short- or long-grain white rice
2 cups (16 fl oz) water
1 cup (8 fl oz) unsweetened coconut cream
2 green chillies, seeded and chopped
2 tablespoons coriander (cilantro) leaves
6 banana leaves*

Wash the rice well and place in a saucepan with the water and coconut cream. Place the saucepan over high heat and bring to the boil. Boil for 8 minutes or until tunnels form in the rice and the liquid is almost absorbed. Remove from the heat.
Stir the chillies and coriander through and pile the mixture onto the banana leaves. Fold over the leaves to encase the rice. Put the parcels in bamboo steamers* and steam for 5 minutes. Serve with coconut chicken curry (see page 120). Serves 6.

lemon and basil pilaf

1 tablespoon oil
2 onions, chopped
2 cloves garlic, crushed
1 tablespoon grated lemon rind
2 cups long-grain rice
4½ cups (36 fl oz) vegetable stock
½ cup basil leaves
cracked black pepper
butter

Place the oil, onion and garlic in a saucepan over medium heat and cook for 4 minutes or until golden. Add the lemon rind and rice. Cook for 3 minutes or until the rice is translucent. Add the stock and basil and allow to simmer for 15 minutes or until the stock is absorbed. Sprinkle well with the pepper and stir a little butter through. Serve with grilled fish and lemon wedges. Serves 4 to 6 as a side dish.

rice in lotus leaves

1 tablespoon oil
3 green onions (scallions), chopped
2 teaspoons grated ginger
1 chicken breast fillet, finely chopped
1 cup chopped Chinese barbecue duck*
½ cup chopped shiitake mushrooms*
3 tablespoons soy sauce
2 teaspoons sugar
4 cups cooked long-grain or glutinous rice
4 dried lotus leaves ▪

Heat the oil in a wok over high heat. Add the onions and ginger and cook for 2 minutes. Add the chicken, duck and mushrooms and cook for a further 4 minutes. Add the soy sauce, sugar and rice and stir well.
Soak the lotus leaves in water until soft, then dry. Place the rice in the lotus leaves and fold over to form a parcel. Place the parcels in bamboo steamers* and steam for 15 minutes. Serves 4.
▪ Available from Chinese supermarkets

soy rice and chicken

2 chicken breasts on the bone
4 tablespoons light soy sauce
2 tablespoons Chinese cooking wine or sherry
1 tablespoon shredded ginger
2½ cups short- or long-grain white rice
3¾ cups (30 fl oz) cold water
6 green onions (scallions), chopped
125g (4 oz) oyster mushrooms*
1 teaspoon cornflour (cornstarch)

Chop the chicken into small pieces and place in a bowl with the soy sauce, wine and ginger. Allow to marinate for 30 minutes.
Wash the rice well under cold water. Place in a large saucepan and pour over the cold water. Bring to the boil and cook for 5 minutes. Reduce heat to low.
Drain the chicken from the marinade and reserve the marinade.
Place the chicken, onions and mushrooms on top of the rice. Cover the pan tightly and cook for a further 15 minutes or until the chicken is tender.
Place the reserved marinade in a saucepan and bring to the boil. Mix the cornflour with a little water to form a smooth paste. Whisk into the marinade and cook for 1 minute. Place the rice and chicken mixture in bowls and top with some sauce. Serves 4.

coconut rice with green chilli

rice in lotus leaves

lemon and basil pilaf

soy rice and chicken

noodles

basics

dried rice

Dried rice noodles range in thickness from thin threads (vermicelli) to flat ribbons or rice sticks. Vermicelli noodles need to be cooked in boiling water for 2 minutes. Thicker noodles need 3–4 minutes. Be sure to test noodles frequently as they should be firm, especially if you are adding them to a stir-fry or cooking them further in a recipe. Always drain well after cooking.

somen

Somen noodles are fine white Japanese noodles made from wheat and water or egg yolk. These noodles are often cooked lightly in boiling water and served cold with a dipping sauce or in soups.

Shanghai

Shanghai noodles are soft, flattish, fresh wheat noodles. You'll find them in the refrigerated section of Asian supermarkets. They have a firm texture when cooked and are used in Chinese soups and stir-fries.

fresh rice

Fresh rice noodles come in a variety of widths and are located in the refrigerated section of Asian and some general supermarkets. Keep them for only a few days in the fridge. To prepare, soak the noodles in hot to boiling water for 1 minute, separating them gently with a fork. Drain and use as the recipe requires.

Hokkien

Hokkien noodles are round, yellow wheat noodles available from the refrigerated section of Asian and general supermarkets. Place the noodles in a bowl and cover with hot to boiling water. Soak for 1–2 minutes or until softened. Drain and use as the recipe requires.

fresh egg

Fresh egg noodles are available in many different thicknesses and shapes in Asian supermarkets. Boil in water for 2 minutes before adding to a stir-fry.

cellophane

Cellophane noodles or bean starch noodles are made from the starch of mung beans and come as vermicelli or as flat, wide noodles. They are difficult to cut and separate when dried, so buy them in small bundles if possible. They need to be soaked in boiling water for 10 minutes or until soft, and then drained. (You can also cut the noodles into shorter lengths.) They can also be deep-fried straight from the packet.

soba

Soba noodles are Japanese noodles made from buckwheat. Sometimes wheat flour is added as well as flavourings such as green tea, shiso leaves and black sesame seeds.

ramen

Ramen noodles are used extensively in Japan, although they are Chinese in origin. They can be purchased fresh but are much more readily available dried. They are used in Japanese noodle soups. The fresh noodles need to be boiled until tender before being added to a soup. Most dried ramen noodles are instant and only need boiling water poured over them to be cooked.

dried egg

Dried egg noodles are available in a variety of thicknesses and need to be boiled until just tender. Drain and add to recipe as required.

udon

Udon noodles are soft, creamy, buff-coloured Japanese wheat flour noodles. They are usually boiled in stock or soup broth and served as an informal, warming snack. They are readily available dried in bundles and you can also find them fresh in some Asian supermarkets.

Hokkien noodles

fresh rice noodles

dried rice noodles

Shanghai noodles

noodles

cellophane noodles

fresh egg noodles

dried egg noodles

dried ramen noodles

fresh ramen noodles

46

dried somen noodles

fresh somen noodles

fresh udon noodles

dried udon noodles

buckwheat soba noodles

barbecue duck and ramen soup   rare beef and cellophane noodle salad

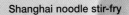

Shanghai noodle stir-fry

barbecue duck and ramen soup

3 cups (24 fl oz) chicken stock
5 cups (40 fl oz) water
8 slices ginger or galangal*
2 red chillies, halved and seeded
2 tablespoons lime or lemon juice
2 stalks lemon grass*
2 coriander (cilantro) roots
1 Chinese barbecue duck,* flesh removed and chopped
4 green onions (scallions), chopped
200g (6½ oz) fresh or 150g (5 oz) dried ramen noodles
beansprouts, chilli and coriander (cilantro) to garnish

Place the stock and water in a saucepan and heat until simmering. Continue simmering and add the ginger, chillies and lime juice. Bruise the lemon grass and coriander with the back of a cleaver to release the flavours and add to the saucepan. Allow to simmer for 20 minutes.
Strain the liquid and return to the saucepan. Add the duck and onions and heat through.
Boil the ramen noodles in a separate saucepan for 3–5 minutes or until tender. Drain. Add the noodles to the soup and simmer for 5 minutes. Ladle the soup and noodles into bowls and garnish with the beansprouts, chilli and coriander. Serves 4 as a main or 6 as a starter.

rare beef and cellophane noodle salad

500g (1 lb) thick rump steak
200g (6½ oz) cellophane noodles
1 green mango, peeled
½ cup Thai basil* leaves
½ cup mint leaves
⅓ cup coriander (cilantro) leaves
dressing
4 tablespoons lime juice
3 tablespoons soy sauce
2 tablespoons brown sugar
1 green chilli, seeded and chopped

Heat a grill (broiler) or frying pan on high for 2 minutes. Cook the steak for 1–2 minutes on each side or until the juices are sealed in and the meat is cooked medium rare. Set aside.
Place the noodles in boiling water and allow to stand for 5 minutes. Drain. Chop the mango finely and combine with the noodles, basil, mint and coriander.
To make the dressing, place the lime juice, soy sauce, sugar and chilli in a bowl and mix to combine.
Slice the steak thinly and toss with the noodle mixture and dressing. To serve, pile onto plates. Serves 4.

Shanghai noodle stir-fry

500g (1 lb) fresh thick Shanghai noodles
2 teaspoons sesame oil
1 tablespoon oil
4 green onions (scallions), chopped
½ Chinese cabbage,* shredded
1 chicken breast, thinly sliced
250g (8 oz) lean pork loin, thinly sliced
150g (5 oz) bok choy,* chopped
3 tablespoons soy sauce
1 tablespoon hoisin sauce*

Place the noodles in a wok or saucepan of boiling water and allow to boil for 5 minutes. Drain and rinse in cold water. Heat the oils in a wok. Add the onions and cook for 1 minute. Add the noodles and stir-fry for 4 minutes. Add the remaining ingredients and cook for 5–7 minutes or until cooked through. Serve with chilli sauce. Serves 4.

chilled soba noodle salad

300g (10 oz) dried buckwheat soba noodles
1 cucumber, chopped
1 tablespoon shredded ginger
2 tablespoons black sesame seeds■
4 green onions (scallions), chopped
125g (4 oz) sashimi tuna,* thinly sliced
dressing
4 tablespoons Japanese soy sauce
4 tablespoons mirin*
wasabi* to taste

Place the noodles in a large saucepan of boiling water. When the water returns to the boil, add 1 cup (8 fl oz) cold water and bring to the boil again. Cook for 8 minutes or until the noodles are tender. Rinse under cold water and drain well. Place in the fridge to cool.
Toss the cold noodles with the cucumber, ginger, sesame seeds and onions. Place the noodles on plates and top with the tuna.
To make the dressing, place the soy sauce, mirin and wasabi in a bowl and whisk to combine. Serve the dressing in small bowls next to each salad. Serves 4 as a main or 6 as a starter.
■ Available from Asian supermarkets.

chilled soba noodle salad

rice noodle pancakes

udon noodles in miso broth

Hokkien noodles with seared scallops

somen noodles with chilli and lime dipping sauce

Thai rice noodles

egg noodles with Chinese barbecue pork

rice noodle pancakes

300g (10 oz) fresh thin rice noodles
2 green chillies, seeded and chopped
2 teaspoons shredded ginger
2 tablespoons chopped coriander (cilantro)
2 tablespoons sesame seeds
oil for shallow-frying
350g (11¼ oz) pork fillet, sliced very thinly
2 tablespoons soy sauce
2 teaspoons grated lime rind
hoisin sauce*

Place the noodles in a bowl, pour over boiling water and
allow to stand for 3 minutes. Drain well. Place on paper
towel to drain away any excess water.
Combine the noodles with the chillies, ginger, coriander
and sesame seeds. Heat 1 cm (½ inch) oil in a frying pan
over medium heat. Place spoonfuls of noodle mixture in the
pan and flatten with a spatula. Cook the pancakes for
2–3 minutes each side or until golden and crisp. Drain on
paper towel and repeat with the remaining mixture.
Place the pork, soy sauce and lime rind in a shallow
dish. Allow to marinate for 10 minutes. Char-grill (broil)
the pork on a preheated hot grill (broiler) for 3–4 minutes
or until cooked medium.
To serve, place the pancakes in a stack on a serving plate.
Top with the slices of pork and drizzle with hoisin sauce.
Serves 6.

udon noodles in miso broth

6 cups (48 fl oz) cold water
8cm (3 inch) piece kombu*
5 tablespoons dried bonito flakes*
2 tablespoons red miso*
250g (8 oz) dried udon noodles
300g fresh asparagus, trimmed and halved
150g (5 oz) firm tofu, chopped
2 green onions (scallions), chopped

Place the water and kombu in a saucepan and slowly bring
to the boil. As soon as the water boils, remove the kombu.
Remove the water from the heat and add the bonito flakes.
Return the liquid to the heat and bring to the boil. As soon
as the liquid boils, remove from the heat and set aside for
1 minute. Strain through a fine sieve or muslin.
Place the strained liquid in a saucepan and bring to the
boil. Add a little of the liquid to the miso and mix until
smooth. Add the miso to the pan. Add the noodles and
asparagus. Boil for 6–8 minutes or until al dente. Stir
the tofu and onions through the noodle mixture. Serve
immediately. Serves 4 as a main or 6 as a starter or
side dish.

Hokkien noodles with seared scallops

350g (11¼ oz) Hokkien noodles
2 teaspoons sesame oil
8 green onions (scallions), trimmed and halved
1 tablespoon shredded ginger
200g (6½ oz) snake beans, trimmed and chopped
250g (8 oz) gai larn,* chopped
3 tablespoons oyster sauce
2 tablespoons sweet chilli sauce
1 tablespoon chilli oil*
12 scallops
lime wedges

Place the noodles in a bowl and cover with boiling water.
Allow to stand for 2 minutes. Drain well.
Heat the oil in a wok or frying pan over high heat. Add the
onions and ginger and stir-fry for 2 minutes. Add the snake
beans, gai larn, oyster sauce and sweet chilli sauce and
cook for 2 minutes. Add the noodles and cook for a further
3 minutes or until heated through.
Place the noodles in bowls. Heat the chilli oil in a wok
or frying pan over high heat. Add the scallops and cook
for 10–20 seconds on each side or until just seared.
To serve, place the scallops on top of the noodles and
serve with lime wedges. Serves 4.

somen noodles with chilli and lime dipping sauce

350g (11¼ oz) dried somen noodles
12 cooked medium prawns (shrimp), shelled
cracked black pepper
chilli and lime dipping sauce
1 teaspoon sesame oil
2 red chillies, seeded and chopped
2 teaspoons grated ginger
4 tablespoons soy sauce
2 tablespoons sweet sherry
3 tablespoons lime juice
2 tablespoons brown sugar

Place the noodles in a saucepan of boiling water. Allow
to boil for 10 minutes or until al dente. Drain, rinse in
cold water and place in the fridge until cold.
To make the dipping sauce, place the oil in a saucepan
over medium heat. Add the chillies and ginger, and cook
for 1 minute. Remove the pan from the heat and stir
the soy sauce, sherry, lime juice and sugar through. Toss
the prawns in a little pepper.
To serve, place the noodles and prawns on plates. Spoon
the dipping sauce into small bowls and place one on each
plate. Serves 4.

Thai rice noodles

350g (11¼ oz) fresh or 150g (5 oz) dried rice noodles
2 teaspoons oil
4 green onions (scallions), chopped
1 red chilli, seeded and chopped
1 small piece ginger, shredded
1 chicken breast fillet, chopped
12 green (raw) prawns (shrimp), shelled and deveined
4 tablespoons soy sauce
2 teaspoons fish sauce*
2 tablespoons brown or palm sugar*
100g (3¼ oz) firm tofu, chopped
2 tablespoons lemon or lime juice
100g (3¼ oz) beansprouts
2 tablespoons mint leaves
2 tablespoons basil leaves

Prepare the noodles following the instructions on page 44.
Place the oil in a wok or frying pan over high heat. Add
the onions, chilli and ginger and stir-fry for 2 minutes.
Add the chicken and prawns and cook for 3 minutes or
until the chicken is golden.
Add the soy sauce, fish sauce, sugar and noodles. Cook
for 2 minutes. Add the tofu, lemon juice, beansprouts,
mint and basil. Cook for 1 minute. Serve immediately
with extra lime or lemon wedges. Serves 4.

egg noodles with Chinese barbecue pork

350g (11¼ oz) fresh or 200g (6½ oz) dried egg noodles
1 tablespoon sesame oil
2 onions, chopped
1 green capsicum (bell pepper), chopped
200g (6½ oz) bok choy*
350g (11¼ oz) Chinese barbecue pork,* sliced
3 tablespoons dark soy sauce
2 tablespoons sweet white cooking wine
¼ cup (2 fl oz) chicken stock
chilli sauce

Prepare the noodles following the instructions on page 44.
Heat the oil in a wok or frying pan over high heat. Add the
onions and cook for 5 minutes or until golden. Add the
capsicum, bok choy and pork and stir-fry for 2 minutes.
Add the noodles, soy sauce, wine and stock and cook for
4 minutes or until heated through. Serve in deep bowls
with chilli sauce on the side. Serves 4.

Asian noodle and herb soup

200g (6¼ oz) rice vermicelli
3 tablespoons Vietnamese mint* leaves
3 tablespoons basil leaves
1 cup beansprouts or pea shoots
6 cups (48 fl oz) chicken stock
6 kaffir lime* leaves
2 red chillies, seeded and chopped
4 slices ginger
3 chicken breast fillets

Cook the vermicelli in boiling water until tender. Drain.
Divide between 6 serving bowls and top with the mint,
basil and beansprouts.
Place the stock, lime leaves, chillies and ginger in a
saucepan and bring to the boil. Add the chicken and
poach for 4 minutes or until cooked through. Remove
the chicken and shred the meat. Continue to simmer
the stock for 5 minutes.
To serve, place the shredded chicken on top of the
noodles in bowls and ladle the hot stock over. Serve
immediately. Serves 6.

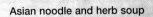
Asian noodle and herb soup

vegetables

basics

steaming

Steaming is an easy way to cook vegetables and almost all vegetables can be steamed. Steaming vegetables retains their water-soluble vitamins. Starchy vegetables such as potatoes aren't generally suitable for steaming. When steaming, make sure that vegetables are cut into equal-sized pieces so they cook evenly. To steam vegetables, place them in a bamboo* or metal steamer, place a lid on the steamer and put over a saucepan of boiling water. Steam is extremely hot, so be careful not to overcook vegetables. Serve vegetables soon after steaming.

mashing

Mashing or pureeing is a great way to serve a variety of vegetables including potatoes, parsnip, pumpkin and celeriac (celery root). Food processors are often used to puree vegetables, although processing potatoes this way gives them a starchy, gluey texture, so these are best done with a masher or fork. Adding milk or cream when mashing will thin the mash as well as give it richness. Adding butter to mash also gives richness. Be sure to purchase varieties of potatoes that are good for mashing. Pepper, roast garlic, herbs and freshly ground spices are great to add to mashed or pureed vegetables. For good mashed potato, boil peeled potatoes until they are soft. Drain and put them warm on the stove top while mashing. Add a teaspoon of butter for each large potato to be mashed. Mash potatoes with a masher or fork and add enough milk to form a smooth mash. Season with any extra flavours and serve.

stir-frying

Stir-frying is an easy and quick way to prepare vegetables. The secret to stir-frying is to have the pan or wok very hot and the vegetables cut into similar-sized pieces so they cook evenly. Starchy vegetables are not suitable for stir-frying. Stir-fried vegetables should be flavoured near the end of the cooking time. For simple stir-fried vegetables, heat some sesame oil over high heat in a wok or frying pan. Add assorted vegetables and stir-fry for 3–5 minutes. Complete the dish with a squeeze of lemon and cracked black pepper. Serve immediately.

roasting

A variety of vegetables can be roasted, including root vegetables, onions, pumpkin and capsicums (bell peppers). Some vegetables (pumpkin and sweet potato/kumara) are better peeled and others (beetroot/beet and potatoes) just need a good scrub before roasting. For even browning, place vegetables in a baking dish and drizzle oil over them. Shake the dish well to coat the vegetables. For salt and rosemary potatoes, add 2 teaspoons of sea salt and 1 tablespoon of rosemary leaves. Bake at 200ºC (400ºF) for 45 minutes to 1 hour or until the potatoes are golden.

char-grilling

Capsicum (bell pepper), zucchini (courgette), eggplant (aubergine) and fennel are just a few of the vegetables that are great for char-grilling (broiling). The most important rule when char-grilling is to brush the vegetables, not the char grill (broiler), with oil. Greasing the char grill will cause a lot of smoke during the cooking process. Char-grill vegetables on both sides until tender. Pour a dressing over to marinate or serve vegetables with grilled or roast meat.

mashing

steaming

char grilling

stir frying

roasting

vegetables

baked celeriac and blue cheese

Chinese greens in oyster sauce

tomato, smoked mozzarella and oregano pizza

baked celeriac and blue cheese

500g (1 lb) celeriac (celery root), peeled and sliced
1/2 cup chopped roasted hazelnuts
3 potatoes, peeled and sliced
2 cups (16 fl oz) cream (pouring or single)
150g (5 oz) blue cheese, crumbled
1 teaspoon caraway seeds

Preheat the oven to 200°C (400°F). Layer the celeriac, hazelnuts and potatoes in a greased ovenproof dish. Pour over the cream and bake for 40 minutes. Sprinkle over the cheese and caraway seeds and bake for 15 minutes. Serve with roast meat. Serves 4.

Chinese greens in oyster sauce

250g (8 oz) gai larn*, cut into short lengths
150g (5 oz) choy sum*, cut into short lengths
2 teaspoons sesame oil
1 teaspoon grated ginger
3 tablespoons oyster sauce
3 tablespoons chicken stock
1 tablespoon soy sauce
2 teaspoons sugar

Place the gai larn and choy sum in boiling water for 30 seconds. Drain and set aside.
Heat the oil in a wok or frying pan over high heat. Add the ginger and cook for 1 minute.
Add the remaining ingredients and cook for 2 minutes. Add the vegetables and toss for 1 minute or until heated through. Serve immediately. Serves 4.

tomato, smoked mozzarella and oregano pizza

1 quantity pizza dough*
300g (10 oz) smoked mozzarella cheese, sliced
2 green tomatoes, sliced
2 red tomatoes, sliced
2 cloves garlic, sliced
3 tablespoons oregano leaves
olive oil
1/2 cup shaved parmesan cheese

Heat 2 baking trays in a preheated 180°C (350°F) oven. Divide the dough into 4 pieces and roll until 3mm (1/8 inch) thick. Top with the mozzarella and green and red tomatoes. Sprinkle over the garlic, oregano, oil and parmesan. Slide onto the preheated baking trays. Bake for 25 minutes or until the crust is golden. Serves 4.

vegetable pies

1 quantity or 250g (8 oz) shortcrust pastry*
750g (1 1/2 lb) potatoes, chopped
2 tablespoons butter
1/2 cup (4 fl oz) milk
1/2 cup grated cheddar cheese
300g (10 oz) pumpkin, chopped
300g (10 oz) orange sweet potato (kumara), chopped
200g (6 1/2 oz) broccoli, chopped
120g (4 oz) green beans, trimmed and halved
2 tablespoons chopped basil
1/2 cup grated parmesan cheese

Roll out the pastry on a lightly floured surface until 3mm (1/8 inch) thick. Line 6 small pie dishes with pastry and refrigerate until required.
Preheat the oven to 200°C (400°F). Cook the potatoes in a saucepan of boiling water until soft. Drain and mash with the butter and milk. Stir through the cheddar cheese. Boil the pumpkin and sweet potato until soft. Drain and mix with the mashed potato, broccoli, beans and basil. Spoon the mixture into the pastry cases and top with the parmesan. Bake for 30 minutes or until the pies are golden. Serves 6.

rice paper rolls

12 rice paper rounds*
1 cup snow pea (mange tout) shoots
1/2 cup shredded carrot
1/2 cup shredded raw beetroot (beet)
125g (4 oz) enoki mushrooms*
1/4 cup mint leaves
1/4 cup Thai basil* leaves
dipping sauce
2 tablespoons lime juice
2 tablespoons chilli sauce
2 teaspoons brown sugar

Soak the rice paper rounds a few at a time in warm water until soft. Place a small pile of snow pea shoots, carrot, beetroot, mushrooms, mint and basil on each rice paper. Fold and roll to enclose.
To make the dipping sauce, combine the lime juice, chilli sauce and sugar. Serve the rice paper rolls with the dipping sauce. Serves 4.

vegetable pies

roast capsicum soup

sweet potato soup

spinach, lemon and lentil soup   onion and fennel soup

roast capsicum soup

5 red capsicums (bell peppers), quartered
1 tablespoon oil
2 cloves garlic
2 red onions, chopped
4 tomatoes, peeled and chopped
4 cups (32 fl oz) chicken stock
cracked black pepper

Place the capsicum quarters under a hot grill (broiler), skin-side up, and grill (broil) until the skins are black and charred. Put the capsicums in a plastic bag, seal and allow to stand for 5 minutes. Remove from the bag and peel away skins.
Heat the oil in a frying pan over medium heat. Add the garlic and onions and cook for 4 minutes or until soft and golden. Add the tomatoes and cook for 5 minutes or until very soft. Place the capsicums and tomato mixture in a blender or food processor and process until smooth. Return the mixture to the pan and add the stock. Cook over medium heat for 5 minutes or until the soup is hot. Sprinkle with pepper and serve with toast. Serves 4.

sweet potato soup

1kg (2 lb) orange sweet potato (kumara), peeled and chopped
2 teaspoons oil
2 tablespoons shredded ginger
2 teaspoons cumin seeds
2 red chillies, chopped
2 stalks lemon grass,* finely chopped
2 cups (16 fl oz) vegetable stock
2 cups (16 fl oz) coconut milk
1 tablespoon palm* or brown sugar
1/2 cup coriander (cilantro) leaves

Place the sweet potato in a saucepan of boiling water and cook for 5 minutes or until tender. Drain and set aside. Heat the oil in a saucepan over medium heat. Add the ginger, cumin seeds, chillies and lemon grass and cook for 3 minutes. Place the sweet potato and spice mixture in a food processor or blender and process with a little of the stock until smooth.
Place the sweet potato mixture in a saucepan over medium heat. Add the remaining stock, coconut milk and palm sugar. Stir until the soup is simmering and hot. Stir through the coriander and serve. Serves 4.

spinach, lemon and lentil soup

350g (11 1/4 oz) green lentils
1 tablespoon olive oil
3 leeks, finely chopped
4 cloves garlic, crushed
3 potatoes, peeled and chopped
3 bay leaves
4 sprigs thyme
4 sprigs oregano
4 cups (32 fl oz) vegetable stock
8 cups (64 fl oz) water
500g (1 lb) English spinach, trimmed and chopped
1/3 cup (2 3/4 fl oz) lemon juice

Place the lentils in a bowl, cover with cold water and allow to stand for 2 hours.
Heat the oil in a large saucepan over medium heat. Add the leeks and garlic and cook for 6 minutes or until golden and soft. Add the potatoes, bay leaves, thyme, oregano, stock, water and drained lentils and simmer for 40 minutes or until the lentils are soft.
Add the spinach and lemon juice and cook for 1 minute. Serve the soup with grilled Turkish bread or flat bread. Serves 6.

onion and fennel soup

1 tablespoon oil
6 onions, chopped
2 tablespoons chopped thyme
1 tablespoon rosemary leaves
4 cups (32 fl oz) beef or vegetable stock
2 cups (16 fl oz) water
350g (11 1/4 oz) fennel, sliced
shaved parmesan cheese
cracked black pepper

Place the oil in a saucepan over low heat. Add the onions, thyme and rosemary and cook for 10 minutes or until the onions are soft and well browned. Add the stock, water and fennel and simmer for 8 minutes.
To serve, place the soup in bowls and top with parmesan and pepper. Serves 4.

rice paper rolls

eggplant and chickpea salad

onion tart   shiitake mushroom omelette

baby spinach, cheese and olive pie

stir-fried beans with lemon and cashews

asparagus with sweet sake and ginger

sweet potato and sage tart

eggplant and chickpea salad

2 eggplants (aubergines), chopped
salt
3 tablespoons olive oil
3 cloves garlic, sliced
2 teaspoons ground coriander
1 teaspoon cardamom seeds
1 teaspoon ground cinnamon
2 cups cooked chickpeas (garbanzos)
1/2 cup chopped flat-leaf (Italian) parsley
200g (6½ oz) baby English spinach leaves
dressing
1/2 cup (4 fl oz) yoghurt
2 tablespoons chopped mint
2 teaspoons honey
2 teaspoons ground cumin

Place the eggplant chunks in a colander, sprinkle with salt and allow to drain for 20 minutes. Rinse and pat dry with paper towel.
Heat the oil in a frying pan over high heat. Add the garlic, coriander, cardamom and cinnamon and cook for 1 minute. Add the eggplant and cook, stirring, for 3 minutes or until golden. Add the chickpeas and cook for 3 minutes or until heated through. Stir through the parsley and remove the pan from the heat.
To make the dressing, combine the yoghurt, mint, honey and cumin.
To serve, place the spinach on plates. Top with the eggplant and chickpea mixture, and drizzle with dressing. Serves 4.

onion tart

5 onions, sliced
2 tablespoons olive oil
2 tablespoons butter
3 tablespoons sage leaves
250g (8 oz) ready-prepared puff pastry
150g (5 oz) soft goat's cheese
cracked black pepper

Preheat the oven to 200°C (400°F). Place the onions, oil, butter and sage in a saucepan over low heat. Cook for 12 minutes or until soft and golden.
Roll out the pastry on a lightly floured surface until 3mm (1/8 inch) thick. Trim to an 18 x 25cm (7 x 10 inch) rectangle and place on a baking tray. Spread the goat's cheese over the pastry and top with pepper.
Spoon the onions over the goat's cheese. Bake for 20 minutes or until the pastry is puffed and golden. Serve with a salad of mixed greens. Serves 4.

shiitake mushroom omelette

2 teaspoons sesame oil
125g (4 oz) shiitake mushrooms,* sliced
1/2 cup chopped chives
1 teaspoon miso*
1/4 cup (2 fl oz) boiling water
5 eggs, lightly beaten
cracked black pepper

Heat the oil in a wok or frying pan over medium heat. Add the mushrooms and chives and stir-fry for 2 minutes. Dissolve the miso in the water and add to the pan. Continue stir-frying until the liquid has evaporated. Pour the eggs over the mushrooms and swirl the mixture around the sides of the wok to form a thin omelette. Cook for 1 minute. Remove from the pan and roll. Top with pepper and serve. Serves 2.

baby spinach, cheese and olive pie

125g (4 oz) baby spinach leaves
125g (4 oz) small sorrel* leaves
1 tablespoon butter
6 green onions (scallions), chopped
freshly grated nutmeg
375g (12 oz) ricotta cheese
1/3 cup grated parmesan cheese
1/4 cup chopped parsley
1/4 cup chopped mint
1/2 cup chopped pitted olives
3 eggs, lightly beaten
8 sheets filo pastry
olive oil

Preheat the oven to 180°C (350°F). Place the spinach and sorrel in a frying pan over medium heat and stir until wilted. Drain well. Place the butter in a frying pan over medium heat. Add the onions and nutmeg and cook for 2 minutes. Combine the greens, ricotta, parmesan, parsley, mint, olives and eggs in a large bowl. Brush the filo with a little olive oil and place the sheets, overlapping and overhanging, around a large pie dish. Pour in the filling, fold over any excess filo and bunch the pastry to make a rim around the pie. Bake for 35 minutes or until the pie is set. Serves 6.

asparagus with sweet sake and ginger

2 teaspoons oil
2 tablespoons shredded ginger
4 green onions (scallions), chopped
1/2 cup (4 fl oz) sweet sake* or mirin*
2 tablespoons light soy sauce
1 tablespoon oyster sauce
500g (1 lb) fresh asparagus
1 tablespoon black sesame seeds■
pickled ginger to serve

Heat the oil in a wok or frying pan over medium heat. Add the ginger and onions and stir-fry for 2 minutes. Add the sake, soy sauce and oyster sauce and cook for 2 minutes. Add the asparagus and stir-fry for 3–4 minutes or until bright in colour. Stir through the sesame seeds. Serve in deep bowls with pickled ginger. Serves 4.
■ Available from Chinese supermarkets.

stir-fried beans with lemon and cashews

1 tablespoon butter
1/2 cup unsalted cashew nuts, chopped
200g (6 1/2 oz) green beans, trimmed
150g (5 oz) snake beans, halved
150g (5 oz) yellow beans, trimmed
1/3 cup (2 3/4 oz) lemon juice
2 tablespoons palm* or brown sugar
1 tablespoon light soy sauce
2 tablespoons mint leaves

Heat the butter in a frying pan or wok over medium heat. Add the cashews and stir-fry for 2 minutes. Add the beans and stir-fry for 3 minutes or until crisp but tender. Add the lemon juice, sugar, soy sauce and mint and cook for 1 minute or until heated through. Serve with couscous. Serves 4.

sweet potato and sage tart

1 quantity or 250g (8 oz) shortcrust pastry*
750g (1 1/2 lb) orange sweet potato (kumara)
1/2 cup (4 fl oz) sour cream
3 eggs
2 tablespoons chopped sage
1 tablespoon honey
2 teaspoons ground cumin
1 teaspoon grated nutmeg
cracked black pepper
sage leaves, extra

Roll out the pastry on a lightly floured surface until 3mm (1/8 inch) thick. Place in a 23cm (9 inch) tart tin and refrigerate until required.
Preheat the oven to 200°C (400°F). Cook the sweet potato in a saucepan of boiling water until soft. Drain and place in a food processor. Add the sour cream and process until smooth. Stir through the eggs, chopped sage, honey, cumin, the nutmeg and the pepper.
Spoon the mixture into the pastry shell and sprinkle over the extra sage leaves. Bake for 35 minutes or until the pastry is golden and the filling is set. Allow the tart to stand for 5 minutes before cutting into wedges. Serve warm or cool. Serves 6.

pumpkin gnocchi

750g (1 1/2 lb) pumpkin, peeled and chopped
2 tablespoons butter
1 1/4 cups plain (all-purpose) flour
1 egg yolk
cracked black pepper
shaved parmesan cheese
butter sauce
125g (4 oz) butter
2 tablespoons thyme leaves

Place the pumpkin in a saucepan of boiling water and cook until soft. Drain and press through a sieve. Return to the saucepan and add the butter. Cook, stirring, over low heat until the pumpkin has thickened and dried. Remove from the heat and stir through the flour, egg yolk and pepper. The mixture should be a soft dough. Roll tablespoons in the palm of your hand to form a flat disk. Press with a fork on one side to indent.
To make the sauce, place the butter and thyme in a saucepan over low heat and simmer until golden.
Cook the gnocchi a few at a time in a saucepan of boiling water until they rise to the surface of the water.
To serve, top the gnocchi with some butter sauce, parmesan and pepper. Serves 4.

pumpkin gnocchi

Jerusalem artichoke hummus with rosemary bruschetta

leek and cheddar soufflé

zucchini pancakes with double brie

stir-fried pumpkin with red curry

Jerusalem artichoke hummus with rosemary bruschetta

350g (11¼ oz) Jerusalem artichokes, scrubbed
2 tablespoons butter
¾ cup (6 fl oz) milk
1½ cups cooked chickpeas (garbanzos)
1 teaspoon ground cumin
2 tablespoons lemon juice
1 clove garlic, crushed
rosemary bruschetta
1 loaf wood-fired bread
olive oil
6 sprigs rosemary

Place the Jerusalem artichokes in a saucepan of boiling water and cook for 5 minutes or until tender. Drain. Place in a food processor with the butter and milk and process until smooth. Add the chickpeas, cumin, lemon juice and garlic and process until smooth.
To make the rosemary bruschetta, slice the bread thinly and brush with a little olive oil. Sprinkle with rosemary, place under a hot grill (broiler) and cook until crisp. Serve with the hummus. Serves 4 to 6.

zucchini pancakes with double brie

2 cups grated zucchini (courgette)
2 eggs
3 tablespoons melted butter
¾ cup plain (all-purpose) flour
⅓ cup grated parmesan cheese
cracked black pepper
½ teaspoon grated nutmeg
200g (6½ oz) double-cream brie cheese
100g (3¼ oz) semi-dried tomatoes
2 tablespoons chopped chives

Squeeze the zucchini to remove any excess liquid. Place in a bowl with the eggs, butter, flour, parmesan, pepper and nutmeg. Mix until smooth. Heat a non-stick frying pan over medium heat. Add spoonfuls of the mixture and cook for 2 minutes on each side or until the pancakes are golden. Keep the pancakes warm and repeat with the remaining mixture.
To serve, spread a little double-cream brie over the pancakes and top with the semi-dried tomatoes and chives. Serves 4.

leek and cheddar soufflé

2 tablespoons olive oil
3 leeks, chopped
2 tablespoons butter
3 tablespoons plain (all-purpose) flour
1¼ cups (10 fl oz) milk, warmed
¾ cup grated aged cheddar cheese
1 tablespoon lemon thyme leaves
cracked black pepper
3 egg yolks
4 egg whites
1½ cups (12 fl oz) cream (single or pouring)

Preheat the oven to 180°C (350°F). Heat the olive oil in a frying pan over medium heat. Add the leeks and cook for 6 minutes or until golden. Set aside.
Place the butter in a saucepan over medium heat and melt. Add the flour and cook, stirring, for 1 minute. Whisk in the milk and stir until it boils and thickens. Remove from the heat and stir through the cheese, thyme, pepper, leeks and egg yolks.
Beat the egg whites until soft peaks form. Fold through the cheese mixture and spoon into six 1-cup capacity greased soufflé ramekins.* Place in a baking dish and fill the dish with enough water to come halfway up the sides of the ramekins. Bake for 20 minutes or until the soufflés are puffed and set. Remove the baking dish from the oven and allow the soufflés to fall and cool slightly.
To serve, invert onto deep dishes and coat each soufflé with cream. Return to the oven and bake for a further 15 minutes or until puffed and golden. Serve with a rocket (arugula) salad. Serves 6.

stir-fried pumpkin with red curry

1 tablespoon oil
2–3 tablespoons red curry paste*
2 onions, chopped
650g (1 lb 5 oz) pumpkin, peeled and sliced
6 curry leaves*
1½ cups (12 fl oz) coconut milk
3 tablespoons coriander (cilantro) leaves
1 red chilli, chopped
100g (3¼ oz) Thai pea eggplants*
½ cup toasted almonds, roughly chopped

Heat the oil in a frying pan or wok over medium heat. Add the curry paste and onion and cook for 2 minutes. Add the pumpkin and stir-fry for 3 minutes. Add the curry leaves, coconut milk and coriander and allow to simmer for 8 minutes or until the pumpkin is soft. Stir through the chilli, pea eggplants and almonds and cook for 2 minutes. Serve with steamed basmati rice. Serves 4.

salads

basics

Salads come in many different forms and can be served in many ways. A salad makes a great light starter or an accompaniment to a main meal. Salads can also be a meal in themselves when they contain a variety of substantial ingredients as well as leafy greens.

storage

Most salad greens store well if they are washed and a little water is left on the leaves. Wrap greens loosely in a damp cloth and refrigerate. Store them in the vegetable crisper or a cool part of the fridge, not the coldest part. Salad greens have a high water content and therefore are not suitable for freezing.

selection

When selecting lettuce, the leaves should be crisp and tightly layered, especially towards the centre or heart. When selecting soft lettuces such as the butter lettuce, the leaves should be soft but crisp and a good bright green colour. When selecting loose salad leaves such as baby English spinach and rocket (arugula), leaves should be crisp and not wilted and a good dark green colour. Stems should be dry and not discoloured.

preparation

Remove any wilted or damaged outer leaves. Remove leaves individually and trim stems if necessary. Wash under cold running water or soak in cold water for a few minutes. To refresh wilted leaves, place them in a bowl of cold water with a few ice cubes. Remove any excess water by patting dry in a clean tea towel.

variety

Salad greens are available in an extensive range, including baby or young vegetable leaves and Asian varieties. Different salad greens complement different foods. Rocket (arugula) has a definite peppery taste with an intensity ranging from mild to hot. Watercress has a mild peppery taste and wilts quickly, so it needs to be soaked in cold water to refresh. Radicchio has a sharp, bitter flavour that combines well with a strong dressing. Mizuna and endive have a mild flavour and go well with spicy and complex-flavoured food.

serving

To ensure salad leaves stay crisp, pour your dressing over the salad just before serving. Dressings that contain vinegar and lemon juice can make the leaves limp and soft.

mizuna

baby English spinach

radicchio

rocket (arugula)

endive

balsamic dressing

1/3 cup (2³/4 fl oz) balsamic vinegar
1/2 cup (4 fl oz) fruity olive oil
1 tablespoon brown sugar
1/4 cup basil leaves
cracked black pepper

Place all of the ingredients in a saucepan over low heat.
Allow to infuse for 5 minutes. Remove from the heat and
strain into a bottle. Store in the fridge for up to 2 weeks.
Makes 1 cup (8 fl oz).

simple vinaigrette

1/2 cup (4 fl oz) olive oil
1/2 cup (4 fl oz) white wine vinegar
cracked black pepper
sea salt
2 tablespoons wholegrain mustard

Place all of the ingredients in a bowl and whisk to
combine. Store in the fridge for up to 3 weeks.
The dressing will separate on standing. Shake to
recombine. Makes 1 cup (8 fl oz).

Thai dressing

1 tablespoon sesame oil

1/3 cup (2¾ fl oz) light soy sauce

2 tablespoons lime juice

1 tablespoon brown or palm sugar*

2 red chillies, chopped

1 tablespoon coriander (cilantro) leaves

1 teaspoon fish sauce,* optional

Place all of the ingredients in a bowl and mix to combine. Refrigerate for up to 1 week. Makes ½ cup (4 fl oz).

caesar dressing

¾ cup (6 fl oz) whole-egg mayonnaise

½ cup (4 fl oz) sour cream

2 tablespoons wholegrain mustard

1/3 cup grated parmesan cheese

cracked black pepper

4 anchovy fillets, chopped (optional)

Combine all of the ingredients in a bowl and mix well. Store in the fridge for up to 1 week. Makes 1½ cups (12 fl oz).

balsamic octopus salad with basil

warm salad of sautéed black olives

grilled chicken and fig salad

warm red lentil salad

seared oyster salad

rocket and sweet potato salad

sweet fennel and pomegranate salad

warm red lentil salad

2 teaspoons oil
2 teaspoons cumin seeds
2 cloves garlic, crushed
2 teaspoons grated ginger
1½ cups red lentils
3 cups (24 fl oz) vegetable or chicken stock
2 tablespoons chopped mint
2 tablespoons chopped coriander (cilantro)
150g (5 oz) baby spinach leaves
100g (3¼ oz) goat's cheese
cracked black pepper
lime wedges

Heat the oil in a saucepan over medium heat. Add the cumin seeds, garlic and ginger and cook for 2 minutes. Add the lentils and cook for 1 minute. Add the stock 1 cup (8 fl oz) at a time until the liquid has been absorbed; this could take about 20 minutes. Remove the pan from the heat and stir the mint and coriander through the lentils. To serve, place the spinach leaves in bowls and top with the lentils and goat's cheese. Sprinkle with pepper and serve with lime wedges. Serves 4.

rocket and sweet potato salad

450g (14¼ oz) orange sweet potatoes (kumara), peeled
   and sliced
200g (6½ oz) haloumi*
chilli oil*
200g (6½ oz) rocket (arugula) leaves
2 tablespoons Vietnamese mint* leaves
4 green onions (scallions), shredded
dressing
1 red chilli, sliced
2 tablespoons soy sauce
2 tablespoons kaffir lime* or lime juice
2 teaspoons palm* or brown sugar

Brush the sweet potatoes and haloumi with the chilli oil. Cook on a preheated char grill (broiler) for 1–2 minutes on each side or until the sweet potatoes and haloumi are brown. Arrange the rocket, mint and onions on a plate. Top with the sweet potatoes and haloumi. To make the dressing, combine the chilli, soy sauce, lime juice and sugar. Mix well. Pour the dressing over the salad and serve. Serves 4.

seared oyster salad

2 bunches rocket (arugula), trimmed
4 green onions (scallions), shredded
100g (3¼ oz) shaved parmesan cheese
1 cucumber, sliced thinly
24 fresh oysters in half shell
2 tablespoons butter
2 tablespoons oil
1 tablespoon lemon thyme leaves
½ cup rice flour
2 tablespoons lemon juice
cracked black pepper

Arrange the rocket, onions, parmesan and cucumber on plates. Remove the oysters from their shells and set aside. Heat the butter, oil and lemon thyme in a small frying pan over medium heat.
Press both sides of the oysters lightly in the flour and shake off any excess.
Sear the oysters in the hot butter mixture for 5 seconds on each side. Place on the rocket salad. Add the lemon juice and pepper to the pan and simmer for 1 minute. Pour the pan juices over the salad as a dressing and serve immediately. Serves 4.

sweet fennel and pomegranate salad

4 fennel bulbs
seeds from 1 pomegranate
100g (3¼ oz) snow pea (mange tout) leaves or shoots
1 yellow capsicum (bell pepper), sliced
150g (5 oz) goat's cheese, sliced
dressing
3 tablespoons pomegranate juice■
2 tablespoons balsamic vinegar
cracked black pepper

Trim the fennel and remove the tough outer pieces. Cut in half and thinly slice.
Place the fennel, pomegranate seeds, snow pea leaves or shoots, capsicum and goat's cheese in a bowl. Toss the salad gently to combine and place on plates.
To make the dressing, combine the pomegranate juice, vinegar and pepper. Pour over the salad. Serves 4.
■ To make pomegranate juice, halve a fresh pomegranate and squeeze over a sieve.

balsamic octopus salad with basil

500g (1 lb) baby octopus, cleaned and halved
1/4 cup (2 fl oz) balsamic vinegar
1/4 cup (2 fl oz) dry white wine
2 tablespoons honey
cracked black pepper
1 eggplant (aubergine), sliced
1 yellow capsicum (bell pepper), sliced
olive oil
150g (5 oz) curly endive (frisée)
1 cup basil leaves
1 tablespoon oil

Place the octopus, vinegar, wine, honey and pepper in a bowl and mix to combine. Refrigerate for 30 minutes. Brush the eggplant and capsicum with olive oil and cook on a preheated barbecue or char grill (broiler) until soft. Set aside. Drain the octopus and cook on a hot barbecue or char grill for 1–2 minutes or until tender.
To serve, place the endive and half the basil leaves on plates. Top with the eggplant, capsicum and octopus. Heat the oil in a frying pan over medium heat and cook the remaining basil until crisp. Sprinkle the fried basil over the salad. Serves 4.

warm salad of sauteed black olives

2 cups dry salted olives*
2 tablespoons olive oil
4 baby leeks, sliced lengthwise
2 tablespoons chopped oregano
1 tablespoon lemon juice
2 tablespoons balsamic vinegar
200g (6½ oz) baked ricotta cheese
2 roasted yellow capsicums (bell peppers)
cracked black pepper
wood-fired bread

Place the olives in a bowl, cover with water and allow to stand for 30 minutes. Drain.
Place the oil in a frying pan over high heat. Add the leeks and cook until well browned and soft. Add the olives, oregano, lemon juice and vinegar and cook for 3 minutes. Place the olives on a plate and serve with a wedge of baked ricotta, some roasted yellow capsicums, cracked black pepper and crusty wood-fired bread. Serves 4.

grilled chicken and fig salad

2 chicken breast fillets
1 eggplant (aubergine), sliced
olive oil
8 radicchio leaves
6 figs, halved
dressing
1/3 cup (2¾ fl oz) lemon juice
2 tablespoons honey
2 tablespoons marjoram leaves
cracked black pepper

Brush the chicken and eggplant with oil and cook on a preheated char grill (broiler) or barbecue for 2 minutes on each side or until the chicken is cooked through. Set aside. Place the radicchio leaves on plates. Slice the chicken and place on the radicchio.
Top the chicken with eggplant and figs.
To make the dressing, place the lemon juice, honey, marjoram and pepper in a small saucepan over low heat and cook for 2 minutes or until warm. Pour the dressing over the salad and serve. Serves 4.

baby spinach and prosciutto salad

12 slices prosciutto
6 roma tomatoes,* halved
olive oil
cracked black pepper
200g (6½ oz) baby spinach leaves
200g (6½ oz) fresh asparagus, blanched*
1/2 cup shaved parmesan cheese
dressing
2 tablespoons olive oil
2 tablespoons lemon juice
1/4 cup basil leaves, shredded
2 teaspoons brown sugar

Preheat the oven to 180°C (350°F). Place the prosciutto and tomatoes, cut-side up, on a baking dish. Sprinkle with oil and pepper. Bake for 25 minutes or until the prosciutto is crisp and the tomatoes are soft.
Arrange the spinach and asparagus on plates. Top with the tomatoes, prosciutto and parmesan.
To make the dressing, combine the oil, lemon juice, basil and sugar. Pour over the salad and serve. Serves 4.

baby spinach and prosciutto salad

roast pumpkin and couscous salad

green olive and ruby grapefruit salad

Asian tuna salad

rocket, blue cheese and fried pear salad

roast pumpkin and couscous salad

500g (1 lb) pumpkin, sliced
olive oil
sea salt
1 cup couscous
1¼ cups (10 fl oz) boiling water or vegetable stock
2 tablespoons butter
125g (4 oz) green beans, trimmed
⅓ cup mint leaves
dressing
½ cup (4 fl oz) yoghurt
2 teaspoons ground cumin
2 tablespoons chopped mint
1 tablespoon honey

Preheat the oven to 200°C (400°F). Place the pumpkin in a baking dish and toss with a little oil and salt. Bake for 30 minutes or until golden and soft. Set aside.
Place the couscous in a bowl and pour over the boiling water or stock. Add the butter and allow to stand for 5 minutes or until the liquid has been absorbed. Blanch* the beans. Drain and cool. Place the couscous, pumpkin, beans and mint in a bowl and toss to combine.
To make the dressing, combine the yoghurt, cumin, mint and honey. To serve, place the salad on plates and pour over the dressing. Serves 4.

Asian tuna salad

350g (11¼ oz) tuna steak
3 tablespoons soy sauce
1 teaspoon wasabi* paste
1 tablespoon sake* or dry white wine
1 bunch mizuna, trimmed
150g (5 oz) yellow pear tomatoes, halved
1 cucumber, chopped
dressing
2 tablespoons soy sauce, extra
1 tablespoon lime juice
2 teaspoons brown sugar
2 teaspoons sesame oil

Cut the tuna into chunks and combine with the soy sauce, wasabi and sake. Allow to marinate for 10 minutes.
Arrange the mizuna, tomatoes and cucumber on plates.
To make the dressing, combine the soy sauce, lime juice, sugar and oil.
Heat a non-stick frying pan over high heat. Cook the tuna pieces for 5 seconds each side or until seared. Place the tuna on the salad and top with the dressing. Serves 4.

green olive and ruby grapefruit salad

250g (8 oz) green olives
2 ruby grapefruit, sliced
3 tablespoons flat-leaf (Italian) parsley leaves
2 cups watercress sprigs
½ cup roasted hazelnuts
1 avocado, chopped
1 tablespoon pomegranate molasses*
2 tablespoons olive oil
cracked black pepper

Place the olives between paper towels and hit each olive with a mallet or rolling pin to release the stone. Remove the stones from the olive flesh and discard.
Place the olives, grapefruit, parsley, watercress, hazelnuts and avocado on a plate.
Mix together the molasses, oil and pepper. Pour over the salad. Allow to stand for 30 minutes before serving. Serves 4.

rocket, blue cheese and fried pear salad

8 long thin slices bread
olive oil
⅓ cup grated parmesan cheese
2 tablespoons butter
1 tablespoon brown sugar
½ teaspoon cracked black pepper
1 tablespoon coriander (cilantro) leaves
2 pears, peeled and sliced
200g (6½ oz) rocket (arugula) leaves
1 cucumber, sliced
1 red onion, sliced
200g (6½ oz) soft blue cheese
cracked black pepper

Preheat the oven to 180°C (350°F). Brush the bread with a little oil and sprinkle with the parmesan. Place on a baking tray and cook in the oven for 15 minutes or until golden and crisp. Set aside to cool.
Heat the butter in a frying pan over medium heat. Add the sugar, pepper and coriander to the pan and cook for 1 minute. Add the pears and cook for 2 minutes each side or until golden.
To serve, arrange the crisp bread, rocket, cucumber, onion and blue cheese on plates. Top with the pears and pour the pan juices from the pears over the salad. Sprinkle with pepper and serve immediately while the bread is crisp. Serves 4.

meat

basics

Different cuts of meat suit different cooking methods. There are two main methods: dry heat, which includes char-grilling and stir-frying, and moist heat, which includes casseroles and curries. Dry-heat methods need tender cuts while moist-heat methods give much better results with tougher cuts cooked over a longer time.

pan-frying

This is a hot, quick method that requires tender cuts of meat. Ensure the pan is well heated over medium heat for a few minutes before cooking. To avoid oil splattering during cooking, brush the meat, not the pan, with oil.

CUTS TO USE

Beef: rump, fillet, scotch fillet or porterhouse, T-bone, marinated blade.
Lamb: boneless leg steaks, cutlets, loin chops, chump chops, fillet.
Pork: fillet, butterfly steaks, schnitzel, cutlets.

casseroles/currying

These are slow, moist-heat methods that require tougher cuts of meat that tenderise well when simmered in a liquid. Tender cuts are not suitable, as the meat does not break down as well as with tougher cuts. When cooking with a liquid, allow the mixture to simmer but do not allow it to boil.

CUTS TO USE

Beef: blade, chuck, skin on the bone (osso bucco).
Lamb: shoulder, shank.
Pork: forequarter.

selection

Meat should have a moist, red surface with no signs of drying or surface film. The fat should be a creamy white colour and should not be dry. Look for even, well-cut meat free from sinew and excess fat.

storage

Meat is best stored loosely wrapped on a plate in the coldest part of the fridge so the air can circulate around it. If meat is tightly wrapped it will 'sweat'. Meat should be either cooked or frozen within 2–3 days of purchase. When freezing meat, wrap it very tightly or seal it in a plastic bag to prevent air spoilage or freezer burn. Also, don't pile pieces on top of each other but be sure to pack meat as flat as possible so it freezes quickly, which will ensure its texture is not spoiled. Meat should be completely thawed before cooking. Thaw meat on a tray in the fridge.

stir-frying

This is a very hot, quick method of cooking and requires tender cuts of meat or strips of meat that have been marinated. Drain the marinade from the meat before stir-frying and ensure that the frying pan or wok is well heated before adding the meat. Cut the meat into similar-sized pieces to ensure even cooking.

CUTS TO USE

Beef: rump, topside, marinated round.
Lamb: fillet, backstrap or boneless loin.
Pork: fillet, strips from the leg or neck.

roasting

This is a dry-heat method and requires tender cuts to be cooked on high heat quickly or tougher cuts to be cooked more slowly for longer. Meats are often best cooked on a rack in a baking dish with water or stock in the base of the baking dish to keep the meat moist.

CUTS TO USE

Beef: corner piece topside, piece sirloin, piece scotch fillet, standing rib roast, rolled rib roast.
Lamb: leg, shoulder, rack roast, boneless loin, rump piece, boned leg.
Pork: leg, shoulder, loin, rack, fillet, rolled and boned pork loin.

barbecueing or char-grilling

These are hot, quick methods of cooking and require tender cuts or meat that has been marinated. Heat the barbecue plate or char grill (broiler) well and allow the flames to subside.
Drain the marinade from the meat before cooking. Coals should be red and glowing when the meat is placed on the barbecue or char grill to cook.
Oil the food, not the barbecue or char grill, to avoid smoking and splattering.
Char grilling (broiling) can also be done in a char grill pan on the cooktop.

CUTS TO USE

Beef: rump, marinated topside, sirloin, T-bone, scotch fillet or porterhouse, eye fillet, marinated round, marinated blade, marinated ribs.
Lamb: fillet, backstrap or boneless loin, cutlets, marinated leg chops, chump chops, loin chops.
Pork: fillet, cutlets, marinated leg steaks, butterfly steaks, marinated ribs.

baking dishes and racks

lemon thyme

meat thermometer

forks

sage

the perfect steak

4 thick New York or sirloin steaks
oil
cracked black pepper

STEP ONE
Heat a frying pan over medium heat for 5 minutes or until hot. Brush the steaks with a little oil and sprinkle with pepper.

STEP TWO
Place the steaks in the frying pan and do not turn until they are sealed.

STEP THREE
Cook the steaks until the juices rise to the uncooked side, which usually takes about 1½ minutes. Turn the steaks and cook for 1 minute more for medium rare, or for 2 minutes more for medium to well done.

STEP FOUR
Test to see if the steaks are ready by pressing them with tongs. The less movement, the more cooked they are. Avoid cutting the steaks to see if they are cooked, as this only releases the juices and dries them out.

variations

CHILLI STEAK
Sprinkle steaks with dried crushed chillies after brushing with oil.

MUSTARD STEAK
Spread wholegrain mustard over steaks, brush with oil and then cook.

PEPPER STEAK
Press chopped green peppercorns into steaks after brushing with oil.

PESTO STEAK
After turning steaks in pan, spread cooked sides with pesto.

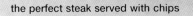

the perfect steak served with chips

simmered veal shanks with wine and lemon

8 x 4cm (1½ inch) pieces veal shank
flour
2 tablespoons olive oil
2 onions, sliced
6 cloves garlic, peeled
2 cups (16 fl oz) dry white wine
2 cups (16 fl oz) chicken stock
rind ½ lemon, cut into strips
4 bay leaves
1 tablespoon chopped thyme
2 baby fennel bulbs, halved
cracked black pepper

Preheat the oven to 180°C (350°F). Toss the veal in the flour and shake off any excess. Heat the oil in a frying pan over high heat. Add the veal to the pan and brown well. Place in the base of a large baking dish. Place the onions and garlic in the frying pan, cook until golden and add to the baking dish.
Add the wine, stock, lemon rind, bay leaves and thyme to the baking dish. Cover and bake for 1½ hours. Add the fennel and bake for a further 45 minutes. Serve the veal in deep plates with the fennel and pan juices, and mashed potato drizzled with olive oil. Serves 4.

Thai beef salad

450g (14¼ oz) rump steak
3 tablespoons soy sauce
2 cloves garlic, crushed
2 tablespoons lime juice
150g (5 oz) assorted lettuce leaves
⅓ cup mint leaves
⅓ cup basil leaves
¼ cup coriander (cilantro) leaves
1 cucumber, sliced
dressing
2 red chillies, chopped
3 tablespoons soy sauce, extra
2 tablespoons lime juice, extra
2 teaspoons palm sugar*
2 kaffir lime* leaves, shredded

Place the steak, soy sauce, garlic and lime juice in a bowl and allow to stand for 10 minutes. Cook the steak on a preheated hot char grill (broiler) for 1–2 minutes each side or until cooked to your liking. Cover the steak and set aside.
Arrange the lettuce, mint, basil, coriander and cucumber on plates. Slice the beef thinly and place on top of the salad. To make the dressing, combine the chillies, soy sauce, lime juice, palm sugar and lime leaves. Pour the dressing over the salad and serve. Serves 4.

Moroccan beef with steamed couscous

1 tablespoon oil
2 onions, chopped
3 cloves garlic, crushed
500g (1 lb) blade or chuck steak, diced
3 tomatoes, peeled and chopped
⅓ cup (2¾ fl oz) lemon juice
1 cinnamon stick
2 teaspoons ground coriander
4 cups (32 fl oz) beef stock
1 tablespoon oregano leaves
2 cups couscous
2 cups (16 fl oz) boiling water
1 tablespoon butter

Heat the oil in a saucepan over medium heat. Add the onions and garlic and cook for 4 minutes or until golden. Add the meat and cook for 5 minutes or until sealed. Add the tomatoes, lemon juice, cinnamon, coriander, stock and oregano and allow to simmer for 45 minutes. Place the couscous, water and butter in a bowl and allow to stand for 2 minutes. Place the couscous in a steamer lined with muslin or cheesecloth. Place the steamer over the simmering beef. Simmer the beef for a further 10 minutes. To serve, place the couscous in bowls and top with the beef. Serves 4.

tamarind and lemon grass beef

1 tablespoon oil
2 stalks lemon grass,* chopped
6 green onions (scallions), chopped
2 green chillies, chopped
500g (1 lb) lean beef strips
3 tablespoons tamarind concentrate*
2 tablespoons lime juice
2 teaspoons fish sauce*
2 teaspoons palm* or brown sugar
1 cup shredded green pawpaw (papaya)

Heat the oil in a wok or frying pan over high heat. Add the lemon grass, onions and chillies and stir-fry for 3 minutes. Add the beef and stir-fry for a further 5 minutes or until well browned. Add the tamarind, lime juice, fish sauce, sugar and pawpaw and stir-fry for a further 4 minutes or until heated through. Serve with rice. Serves 4.

simmered veal shanks with wine and lemon

Moroccan beef with steamed couscous

Thai beef salad

tamarind and lemon grass beef

rare beef and vinegared rice   coconut beef stir fry

seared beef with parmesan and rocket

steaks with red wine mushrooms

rare beef and vinegared rice

400g (12³/₄ oz) piece eye fillet
3 tablespoons soy sauce
1/2 cup (4 fl oz) plum wine or sweet cooking wine
1 tablespoon grated ginger
1 cup short-grain rice
1¹/₂ cups (12 fl oz) water
3 tablespoons seasoned rice wine vinegar
1 tablespoon oil
150g (5 oz) oyster mushrooms*
4 small squares nori,* toasted
4 green onions (scallions), sliced

Place the meat in a shallow dish. Combine the soy sauce, plum wine and ginger. Pour over the meat. Allow to marinate for 30 minutes. Wash the rice well under running water. Place in a saucepan with water and cook over medium heat until the water has almost been absorbed. Remove the pan from the heat, cover and allow to stand for 5 minutes. Place the rice in a bowl and stir through the vinegar. Cover the bowl and keep warm.
Heat the oil in a frying pan over medium heat. Drain the beef and reserve the marinade. Place the beef in a frying pan and cook for 1 minute each side. Remove from the pan and cover. Place the reserved marinade in the frying pan, add the mushrooms and simmer until the liquid has reduced and the mushrooms are soft.
To serve, place the nori on plates and top with the rice and onions. Thinly slice the beef and place on the rice. Top with the mushrooms and reduced marinade. Serves 4.

coconut beef stir-fry

1 tablespoon oil
1 stalk lemon grass,* bruised
4 pieces galangal*
2 red chillies, sliced
3 coriander (cilantro) roots
500g (1 lb) beef strips
8 kaffir lime* leaves, shredded
1 cup (8 fl oz) coconut cream
2 teaspoons fish sauce*
2 teaspoons brown or palm sugar*
1/2 cup Thai basil* leaves

Heat the oil in a wok over medium heat. Add the lemon grass, galangal, chillies and coriander roots and cook for 1 minute. Add the beef and stir-fry for 4 minutes or until well browned. Add the lime leaves, coconut cream, fish sauce and sugar and cook for 2 minutes. Stir through the basil and serve on steamed rice. Serves 4.

seared beef with parmesan and rocket

1 tablespoon olive oil
2 red onions, thickly sliced
500g (1 lb) piece sirloin steak
cracked black pepper
150g (5 oz) rocket (arugula), trimmed
1/2 cup shaved parmesan cheese
3 tablespoons flat-leaf (Italian) parsley
2 tablespoons balsamic vinegar
2 tablespoons olive oil, extra

Heat the oil in a frying pan over medium heat. Add the onions and cook for 5 minutes each side or until well browned. Set aside. Slice the beef into 8 steaks about 1cm (1/2 inch) thick. Sprinkle with pepper. Increase the heat to high. Add the steaks to the pan and cook for 30 seconds to 1 minute each side or until seared.
To serve, toss together the rocket, parmesan, parsley, balsamic vinegar and extra oil. Place 1 piece of steak on each warmed plate. Top with a little of the rocket mixture and another steak. Add more rocket and finish with fried onion. Serves 4.

steaks with red wine mushrooms

1 tablespoon oil
4 thick sirloin or fillet steaks
1 tablespoon butter
4 green onions (scallions), chopped
2 cloves garlic, crushed
100g (3¹/₄ oz) shiitake mushrooms*
100g (3¹/₄ oz) small field mushrooms
1 cup (8 fl oz) beef stock
1 cup (8 fl oz) red wine
1 tablespoon thyme leaves
cracked black pepper
mashed potato to serve

Heat the oil in a frying pan over medium heat. Cook the steaks for 3 minutes each side or until cooked to your liking. While the steaks are cooking, heat the butter in a frying pan over medium heat. Add the onions and garlic and cook for 1 minute. Add the mushrooms and toss for 1 minute. Add the stock, wine, thyme and pepper and allow to simmer until the mushrooms are soft and the sauce is reduced by half.
To serve, place some mashed potato on warmed plates. Top with a steak and pour over the mushrooms and sauce. Serve immediately. Serves 4.

garlic and rosemary studded lamb

1.5kg (3 lb) leg of lamb
4 cloves garlic, sliced
4 sprigs rosemary
¼ cup (2 fl oz) honey

¼ cup Dijon mustard
½ cup (4 fl oz) dry white wine
2 tablespoons chopped mint

STEP ONE
Preheat the oven to 200°C (400°F). Cut small slits in the lamb. Press pieces of garlic and small sprigs of rosemary into the slits.

STEP TWO
Place the lamb on a rack in a baking tray and add 1 cup (8 fl oz) water to the bottom of the baking dish.

STEP THREE
Bake the lamb for 40 minutes. Combine the honey and mustard and brush over the lamb. Bake for a further 10 minutes or until the lamb is cooked to your liking. Remove from the baking dish, cover and set aside.

STEP FOUR
Place the baking dish over medium heat. Add the wine and mint. Stir until the sauce boils. To serve, slice the lamb and serve with mint sauce and roasted vegetables. Serves 4 to 6.

variations

GINGER GLAZE
Use ⅓ cup of ginger marmalade instead of honey.

THYME LAMB
Use 6 sprigs of fresh lemon thyme instead of rosemary.

ORANGE GLAZE
Use ⅓ cup of orange marmalade instead of honey.

OREGANO LAMB
Use 6 sprigs of fresh oregano instead of rosemary.

garlic and rosemary studded lamb

harissa fried lamb fillets

1 tablespoon harissa* or chilli paste
2 tablespoons lemon juice
2 tablespoons chopped mint
350g (11¼ oz) lamb fillets, trimmed
2 eggplants (aubergines)
2 cloves garlic, crushed
⅓ cup (2¾ fl oz) olive oil
½ cup (4 fl oz) yoghurt
2 tablespoons tahini
3 tablespoons lemon juice, extra
4 slices Turkish bread
150g (5 oz) rocket (arugula) leaves

Preheat the oven to 220°C (425°F). Place the harissa, lemon juice, mint and lamb in a bowl and marinate for 20 minutes.
Place the eggplants in a baking dish and bake for 25 minutes or until the skins are charred. Peel away the skins and place the eggplant flesh, garlic, oil, yoghurt, tahini and extra lemon juice in a food processor or blender and process until smooth.
Cook the lamb on a preheated barbecue or char grill (broiler) for 1–2 minutes or until cooked to your liking.
To serve, place the Turkish bread on plates. Top with the rocket and slices of lamb. Serve with the eggplant puree. Serves 4.

slow-simmered lamb shanks

8 lamb shanks, trimmed
3 cups (24 fl oz) beef stock
1 cup (8 fl oz) red wine
6 bay leaves
4 cloves garlic, peeled
8 baby onions, peeled
2 sprigs rosemary
3 sprigs marjoram
1 tablespoon peppercorns

Preheat the oven to 160°C (315°F). Place a frying pan over high heat. Add the lamb shanks and cook for 2 minutes each side or until well browned.
Place the lamb in a baking dish with the stock, wine, bay leaves, garlic, onions, rosemary, marjoram and peppercorns. Cover and bake for 2 hours or until the lamb is very tender.
Serve the lamb shanks in deep bowls with soft polenta or potato and garlic mash. Serves 4.

soft polenta with glazed lamb

4 cups (32 fl oz) hot water
1¼ cups polenta
sea salt and cracked black pepper
65g (2¼ oz) butter
½ cup grated parmesan cheese
½ cup mascarpone
8 lamb cutlets
½ cup (4 fl oz) red wine
½ cup (4 fl oz) beef stock
2 tablespoons quince paste

To cook the polenta, place the water in a heavy-based saucepan over medium heat. Allow to come to a slow simmer. Slowly pour the polenta into the water while whisking to combine. Reduce the heat to as low as possible. Cook the polenta, stirring occasionally with a wooden spoon, for 40–45 minutes. It is cooked when it comes away from the sides of the pan. Stir the salt, pepper, butter, parmesan and mascarpone through the polenta and keep warm.
Place a frying pan over high heat. Add the cutlets and cook for 2 minutes each side or until cooked medium. Remove from the pan and keep warm. Add the wine, stock and quince paste to the pan and simmer for 5 minutes or until the sauce has thickened.
To serve, place the polenta on plates, top with the lamb and spoon over the sauce. Serves 4.

slow-roasted double lamb cutlets

8 small parsnips, peeled and sliced
6 small carrots, peeled and sliced
olive oil
8 double lamb cutlets
½ cup grated parmesan cheese
2 tablespoons wholegrain mustard
2 tablespoons chopped basil
cracked black pepper

Preheat the oven to 200°C (400°F). Place the parsnips and carrots on a baking tray, sprinkle with oil and bake for 30 minutes.
Preheat a large frying pan over medium heat. Add the lamb cutlets and cook for 1 minute on each side or until sealed and brown. Remove from the pan.
Combine the parmesan, mustard, basil and pepper. Spread over the lamb cutlets. Place on a baking tray and reduce the oven temperature to 150°C (300°F). Cook the lamb for 20 minutes or until cooked to your liking.
To serve, place the parsnips and carrots on plates and top with the lamb cutlets. Serves 4.

harissa fried lamb fillets

soft polenta with glazed lamb

slow-simmered lamb shanks

slow-roasted double lamb cutlets

braised lamb and preserved lemon

roast lamb loin with parsnip chips

braised lamb and preserved lemon

1 tablespoon oil
2 cloves garlic, crushed
1 teaspoon cumin seeds
6 green onions (scallions), halved
500g (1 lb) diced lamb
2 tablespoons chopped preserved lemon■
1/3 cup chopped mint
4 bay leaves
1 cinnamon stick
3 cups (24 fl oz) beef stock
4 baby eggplants (aubergines), sliced
yoghurt to serve

Place the oil in a saucepan over medium heat. Add
the garlic, cumin and onions to the pan and cook for
4 minutes. Add the lamb and cook for 5 minutes or until
sealed. Add the preserved lemon, mint, bay leaves,
cinnamon and stock. Cover and simmer for 40 minutes.
Add the eggplants and simmer for a further 10 minutes.
Place the lamb in bowls and serve with yoghurt and a
tomato salad. Serves 4.
■ Available from delicatessens. Remove the flesh and rinse
the rind well before chopping.

roast lamb loin with parsnip chips

500g (1 lb) boneless lamb loin
4 cloves garlic, crushed
2 tablespoons seeded mustard
2 tablespoons chopped mint
1 tablespoon chopped coriander (cilantro)
1 tablespoon olive oil
500g (1 lb) parsnips, peeled
oil for deep-frying
sea salt

Preheat the oven to 200°C (400°F). Trim the lamb of any fat
or sinew. Combine the garlic, mustard, mint, coriander and
oil. Rub the mixture over the lamb and place in a baking
dish. Bake for 10 minutes or until the lamb is cooked to
your liking.
While the lamb is roasting, cut the parsnips into long thin
strips. Deep-fry in hot oil until golden and crisp. Drain on
paper towel and sprinkle with salt.
To serve, slice the lamb thickly and place on plates. Serve
with the parsnip chips. Serves 4.

roast pork with apple stuffing

1.5kg (3 lb) boned pork loin
1 lemon, halved
salt
stuffing
1 tablespoon butter
1 tablespoon oil

1 onion, chopped
3 apples, peeled and sliced
2 tablespoons sage leaves
2 cups fresh breadcrumbs
1/3 cup (2¾ fl oz) milk
cracked black pepper

STEP ONE
To make the stuffing, place the butter and oil in a frying pan over medium heat. Add the onion and cook for 3 minutes or until golden.

STEP TWO
Add the apples and sage to the pan and cook, stirring occasionally, until the apples are golden and soft. Remove the pan from the heat and stir the breadcrumbs, milk and pepper through the onion and apple mixture.

STEP THREE
Score the pork rind at 5mm (1/4 inch) intervals. Spread the stuffing down the middle of the loin of pork. Roll up the pork and tie with cotton string.

STEP FOUR
Preheat the oven to 220°C (425°F). Rub the pork rind with the lemon and salt. Place the pork in a baking dish and cook for 20 minutes. Reduce the heat to 180°C (350°F) and cook for a further 45 minutes or until the pork is cooked. Do not overcook, as pork will become dry and tough. Serves 6.

variations

PEAR STUFFING
Use 3 pears, peeled and sliced, instead of the apples.

APRICOT STUFFING
Use 6 fresh or canned apricots instead of the apples.

BASIL STUFFING
Use 3 tablespoons basil leaves instead of the sage leaves.

ROSEMARY STUFFING
Use 2 tablespoons rosemary leaves instead of the sage leaves.

roast pork with apple stuffing

pork, basil and pepper stir-fry

2 tablespoons oil
2 cloves garlic, chopped
1 tablespoon cracked black pepper
2 red chillies, chopped
500g (1 lb) pork strips
200g (6½ oz) asparagus, halved and trimmed
4 kaffir lime* leaves, shredded
1 cup Thai basil* leaves
2 tablespoons soy sauce
1 mango or 2 nectarines, chopped

Heat the oil in a wok or a large frying pan over high heat. Add the garlic, pepper and chillies and cook for 1 minute. Add the pork and stir-fry for 4 minutes or until well browned. Add the asparagus, lime leaves, basil and soy sauce and stir-fry for 3 minutes. Stir through the mango or nectarine pieces.
Serve in bowls with steamed rice. Serves 4.

pork with ginger and honey

500g (1 lb) pork fillet
2 cloves garlic, crushed
2 tablespoons lemon juice
1 tablespoon oil
2 fennel bulbs, sliced
2 teaspoons oil, extra
4 tablespoons shredded ginger
4 tablespoons honey
½ cup (4 fl oz) Calvados* or brandy

Trim the pork of any fat or sinew. Place in a bowl with the garlic and lemon juice and allow to stand for 5 minutes. Preheat the oven to 180°C (350°F).
Heat the oil in a frying pan over medium heat. Add the pork and cook for 2 minutes each side or until well browned. Place the fennel in a baking dish, place the pork on top of the fennel and cover the dish. Bake for 15 minutes or until the pork is cooked to your liking.
While the pork is cooking, heat the extra oil in a saucepan over medium heat. Add the ginger and cook for 1 minute. Add the honey and Calvados and simmer for 4–5 minutes or until reduced by half.
To serve, slice the pork and place on plates with the fennel. Top with the ginger and honey glaze. Serves 4.

steamed pork buns

1 quantity basic bun mix*
2 teaspoons oil
400g (12¾ oz) Chinese barbecue pork,* diced
1 teaspoon grated ginger
2 green onions (scallions), chopped
2 tablespoons soy sauce
1 tablespoon oyster sauce
½ cup (4 fl oz) chicken stock
2 teaspoons sugar
1 tablespoon cornflour (cornstarch)
2 tablespoons water

To make the filling, place the oil in a hot wok or large frying pan. Add the pork, ginger and onions and stir-fry for 2 minutes. Add the soy sauce, oyster sauce, stock and sugar. Blend the cornflour and water until smooth and add to the wok, stirring until the mixture is very thick. Allow to cool.
Divide the dough into 24 pieces and flatten each piece in the palm of your hand. Place a spoonful of the filling in the centre of each piece and press the edges together to form a bun. Put a small piece of non-stick baking paper under each bun. Leave the buns to rise for 10 minutes. Place in a bamboo steamer* leaving room for the buns to expand. Place the steamer over a wok or large saucepan of rapidly boiling water. Cover and steam for 12 minutes without lifting the lid. Serve. Makes 24 buns.

pork with balsamic figs

4 pork cutlets
2 tablespoons basil oil*
1 tablespoon butter
4 fresh figs, quartered
3 tablespoons balsamic vinegar
⅓ cup (2¾ fl oz) beef stock
2 tablespoons brown sugar
mashed potato to serve

Brush the pork with the basil oil. Heat a frying pan over medium heat. Add the pork and cook for 2–3 minutes each side or until cooked to your liking. Remove from the pan, cover and keep warm.
Add the butter to the pan and heat until melted. Add the figs and cook for 2 minutes or until golden. Remove the figs and set aside. Add the balsamic vinegar, stock and sugar to the pan. Bring to the boil and simmer for 4 minutes or until thickened and reduced. Return the figs to the pan to heat through.
To serve, place piles of mashed potato on plates. Top with the pork, figs and balsamic sauce. Serves 4.

pork, basil and pepper stir fry

steamed pork buns

pork with ginger and honey

pork with balsamic figs

113

poultry

basics

storage

Fresh poultry should be stored loosely covered on a plate in the fridge for up to 2 days. Poultry is susceptible to contamination from salmonella bacteria, which can cause food poisoning. Therefore, care must be taken when storing, preparing and cooking it. Once frozen poultry has thawed, it should be cooked within 1 day.

selection

When choosing poultry, the skin should be a light creamy colour and it should be moist. It should also be unbroken with no dark patches. The breast should be plump and the tip of the breastbone should be pliable. Free-range poultry is usually easily identified by the layer of fat over the breast and its darker or slightly yellower skin colour. The skin of corn-fed poultry has a distinctive yellow tinge. The flesh should have a fresh smell and should be free from any film. Fresh chicken is preferable to frozen. When choosing frozen chicken, be sure that its packaging is well sealed.

preparation

Poultry does not need to be washed before cooking. Wipe the inside cavity with a damp cloth and wipe the skin if necessary. If poultry has been frozen, wipe it with paper towel to remove any excess moisture. When stuffing, be sure to stuff the cavity loosely so the heat can penetrate through the stuffing.

cooking tips

Be sure that poultry is cooked through. To test for readiness, pierce the flesh at the thickest part, usually under the leg, with a fork. The juices should be clear (not pink) when it is cooked. The wings and legs of larger poultry may dry out during long cooking processes, such as roasting. Cover these parts with aluminium foil to protect them from burning.
When cutting poultry to be stir-fried, be sure that the pieces are similar in size, so they cook evenly.

basting

To stop the breast meat of poultry, especially chicken and turkey, from drying out while roasting, mix together some butter, a little pepper and herbs of your choice. Separate the skin from the breast meat and rub the butter mixture under the skin before roasting. This will keep the breast meat moist and tender.

freezing

When freezing poultry, wrap it well in plastic wrap or seal it in a freezer bag, and date and label it. Freeze poultry for no longer than 3 months. Frozen poultry must be thawed in the fridge, not at room temperature. Ensure that poultry is fully defrosted before cooking.

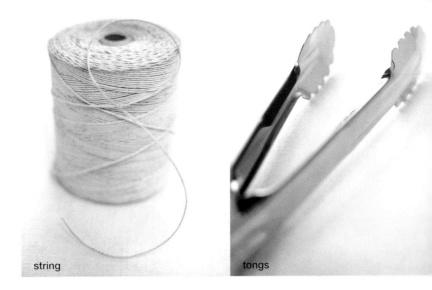

string

tongs

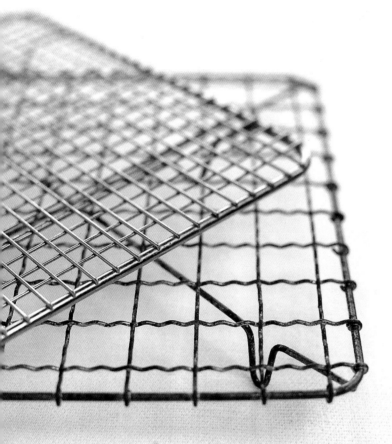

baking racks

basting brush

bay leaves

117

STEP ONE
Wipe and pat dry the chicken. Make sure the cavity is clean and any excess fat is removed. To make the stuffing, place the onion, breadcrumbs, parsley, basil, pepper, lemon rind, egg and milk in a bowl and mix well to combine.

roast chicken

1.8kg (3 lb 10 oz) chicken
6 bay leaves
2 cups (16 fl oz) water
oil
sea salt
stuffing
1 onion, finely chopped
2½ cups fresh breadcrumbs
3 tablespoons chopped parsley
2 tablespoons chopped basil
cracked black pepper
2 teaspoons grated lemon rind
1 egg
½ cup (4 fl oz) milk
gravy
⅓ cup plain (all-purpose) flour
2 cups (16 fl oz) hot water

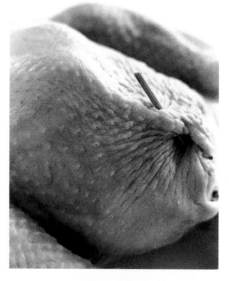

STEP TWO
Press the stuffing into the cavity of the chicken and securely close the cavity with a skewer. Tuck the wings under the chicken and tie the legs together with cotton string.

variations

SUN-DRIED TOMATO STUFFING
Add ⅓ cup chopped sun-dried tomatoes to the stuffing.

OLIVE STUFFING
Add ⅓ cup chopped pitted olives to the stuffing.

TANDOORI CHICKEN
Mix together 3 tablespoons tandoori paste and ½ cup thick plain yoghurt. Spread this mixture over the chicken before roasting.

STEP THREE
Preheat the oven to 200ºC (400ºF). Place the chicken on a rack lined with bay leaves in a baking dish. Place 2 cups (16 fl oz) of water in the bottom of the baking dish. Brush the chicken with a little oil and sprinkle with a little salt. Bake for 1 hour and 15 minutes or until cooked through. Place the chicken on a warmed plate and cover to keep warm.

PEPPER CHICKEN
Mix together 2 tablespoons butter and 1 tablespoon cracked black pepper. Rub this mixture over the chicken before baking.

STEP FOUR
To make the gravy, skim the fat from the pan juices with a spoon. Sprinkle the flour over the pan juices and stir with a fork until smooth. Place the pan over high heat and cook, stirring, for 2 minutes. Add the hot water and mix until smooth. Cook, stirring, until the gravy is simmering and thickened. To serve, carve the chicken and serve with the gravy and roast vegetables. Serves 4.

roast chicken

chicken and lime leaf stir-fry

2 teaspoons sesame oil

6 green onions (scallions), chopped

1 tablespoon shredded ginger

8 kaffir lime* leaves, shredded

4 chicken breast fillets, sliced into strips

2 tablespoons soy sauce

2 tablespoons mirin* or sweet white wine

1 teaspoon red miso*

250g (8 oz) baby bok choy,* chopped

4 tablespoons Thai basil*

Heat the oil in a wok or frying pan over high heat. Add the onions, ginger and lime leaves and stir-fry for 1 minute. Add the chicken strips and stir-fry for 3 minutes or until browned. Add the soy sauce, mirin, miso and bok choy and stir-fry for 3 minutes or until the bok choy is tender. Stir through the basil and serve immediately with steamed rice. Serves 4.

coconut chicken curry

2 teaspoons oil

1 onion, finely chopped

1 tablespoon ginger, shredded

1 stalk lemon grass,* chopped

2–3 tablespoons green curry paste*

6 kaffir lime* leaves, shredded

4 chicken breast fillets, halved

2½ cups (20 fl oz) coconut milk

⅓ cup basil leaves

⅓ cup coriander (cilantro) leaves

Heat the oil in a saucepan over medium heat. Add the onion, ginger and lemon grass and cook for 4 minutes or until the onion is soft and golden. Add the curry paste and lime leaves and cook, stirring, for 2 minutes.
Add the chicken and coconut milk and allow to simmer for 20 minutes. Stir through the basil and coriander. Serve with steamed jasmine rice. Serves 4.

spiced roast chicken

1.6kg (3¼ lb) chicken

60g (2 oz) butter, melted

2 tablespoons soy sauce

2 tablespoons honey

4 cinnamon sticks

4 star anise

4 cardamom pods, bruised

4 cloves garlic, peeled

Preheat the oven to 200°C (400°F). Halve the chicken by cutting down the backbone and breastbone. Place on sheets of non-stick baking paper. Combine the butter, soy sauce and honey and brush well over the chicken. Top the chicken with the cinnamon sticks, star anise, cardamom and garlic. Fold the paper over the chicken and seal. Place in a baking dish and bake for 35 minutes or until tender and cooked through. Serves 4.

roast beetroot with chicken

12 baby beetroot (beets), scrubbed

olive oil

sea salt

2 cinnamon sticks

6 cardamom pods

4 chicken breast fillets, skin on

2 tablespoons butter

1 tablespoon balsamic vinegar

2 teaspoons oregano leaves

200g (6½ oz) small beetroot (beet) tops

150g (5 oz) marinated fetta cheese

Preheat the oven to 180°C (350°F). Place the beetroot in a large baking dish and sprinkle with a little oil and salt. Add the cinnamon and cardamom to the dish and bake for 40 minutes.
Rub the chicken skin with a little salt. Place skin-side down, in a preheated frying pan and brown for 3 minutes. Place the chicken, skin-side up, in the dish with the beetroot and cook for a further 15 minutes.
To serve, place the butter, vinegar and oregano in a small saucepan and heat until bubbling. Place the chicken, beetroot and beetroot tops on plates and sprinkle with the fetta. Spoon the butter mixture over the beetroot tops and serve. Serves 4.

chilli chicken burritos

4 tortillas*

salad greens

2 chicken breast fillets, cooked and shredded

6 red chillies, chopped

½ cup sugar

¼ cup (2 fl oz) water

2 tablespoons lime juice

1 teaspoon cumin seeds

2 tomatoes, chopped

Place the tortillas on a board and top with the salad greens and chicken. Place the chillies, sugar, water, lime juice and cumin seeds in a saucepan and cook over medium heat, stirring, until the sugar is dissolved. Cook for 4 minutes, add the tomatoes and cook until the mixture is thick. To serve, spoon the chilli sauce over the chicken, fold over the tortilla and wrap in a napkin. Serves 4.

chicken and lime leaf stir fry

spiced roast chicken

coconut chicken curry

roast beetroot with chicken

121

chilli chicken burritos

barbecue duck and snake bean stir fry

baked pesto-crusted chicken with rosemary potatoes   roasted green chilli and lime quail

barbecue duck and snake bean stir-fry

1 Chinese barbecue duck*
2 teaspoons sesame oil
4 green onions (scallions), chopped
1 tablespoon shredded ginger
1 cinnamon stick
1 tablespoon grated orange rind
200g (6½ oz) snake beans, halved
3 tablespoons sweet white cooking wine
2 tablespoons light soy sauce

Chop the duck into bite-sized pieces. Heat the oil in a wok or frying pan over high heat.
Add the onions, ginger and cinnamon stick and stir-fry for 3 minutes. Add the orange rind, beans, duck, wine and soy sauce and stir-fry for 5 minutes or until heated through.
Serve the duck and beans in bowls with steamed jasmine rice. Serves 4.

baked pesto-crusted chicken with rosemary potatoes

4 potatoes, thinly sliced
2 tablespoons rosemary leaves
olive oil
4 chicken breast fillets
cracked black pepper
pesto
1 cup basil leaves, firmly packed
2 cloves garlic
⅓ cup (2¾ fl oz) olive oil
⅓ cup grated parmesan cheese
¼ cup pine nuts

Preheat the oven to 200°C (400°F). Layer the potatoes in rounds of 4 on a baking tray. Sprinkle with the rosemary and oil. Bake for 35 minutes or until golden and soft.
To make the pesto, process the basil, garlic, oil, parmesan and pine nuts in a food processor or blender until the mixture is a finely chopped paste.
Place the chicken in a baking dish and spread the tops of each breast with pesto. Reduce the oven to 170°C (325°F) and bake for 15–20 minutes or until the chicken is cooked through.
To serve, place the potato rounds on plates and top with the pesto-crusted chicken. Sprinkle with cracked black pepper. Serve with a witlof (Belgian endive) salad. Serves 4.

roasted green chilli and lime quail

4 quails, halved
2 green chillies, chopped
3 tablespoons lime juice
2 tablespoons honey
½ cup (4 fl oz) dry white wine
2 tablespoons coconut vinegar* or cider vinegar
2 coriander (cilantro) roots
1 stalk lemon grass,* bruised
450g (14¼ oz) orange sweet potato (kumara), peeled
oil for deep-frying
sea salt

Place the quails in a shallow dish. Combine the chillies, lime juice, honey, wine, vinegar, coriander and lemon grass. Pour over the quails and marinate for 30 minutes.
Preheat the oven to 180°C (350°F). Place the quails in a baking dish with the marinade and cover.
Bake for 30 minutes or until the quails are cooked through. While the quails are cooking, slice the sweet potato into long, thin strips. Deep-fry in hot oil until crisp. Drain on paper towel.
To serve, place the sweet potato strips on plates and sprinkle with sea salt. Place the quails on the plates and top with pan juices. Serves 4.

grilled balsamic chicken with limes

3 tablespoons balsamic vinegar
2 cloves garlic, crushed
2 tablespoons olive oil
cracked black pepper
4 chicken breast fillets
4 limes, halved
assorted salad greens
balsamic vinegar, extra

Combine the vinegar, garlic, oil and pepper. Pour over the chicken and allow to marinate for 5 minutes.
Remove the chicken from the marinade. Cook on a preheated barbecue or char grill (broiler) for 1–2 minutes each side or until cooked through. While the chicken is cooking, place the limes on the barbecue or char grill to caramelise.
Arrange the salad greens on plates. Slice the chicken and place on top of the greens. Serve with the grilled limes and sprinkle with the extra balsamic vinegar. Serves 4.

grilled balsamic chicken with limes

peppered tempura chicken with rocket mayonnaise

warm chicken salad

chicken with preserved lemon

chicken, roast tomato and basil sandwiches

peppered tempura chicken with rocket mayonnaise

4 chicken breast fillets, sliced
oil for deep-frying
tempura batter
2 tablespoons cracked black pepper
1 cup plain (all-purpose) flour
1 cup (8 fl oz) soda water
1 egg
rocket mayonnaise
1/2 cup chopped rocket (arugula)
1/2 cup whole-egg mayonnaise
1 tablespoon lime juice

To make the batter, place the pepper, flour, soda water and egg in a bowl and whisk until smooth. Dip the chicken strips into the batter and deep-fry in hot oil for 2 minutes or until the chicken is golden brown. Drain on paper towel.
To make the rocket mayonnaise, process the rocket, mayonnaise and lime juice in a food processor or blender until smooth.
To serve, place the chicken on plates and serve with small bowls of rocket mayonnaise and lime wedges. Serves 4.

chicken with preserved lemon

2 chicken breast fillets on the bone
1 tablespoon olive oil
2 onions, sliced
2 tablespoons sliced preserved lemon■
2 red chillies, halved
2 cloves garlic, crushed
4 sprigs marjoram
1 cup (8 fl oz) white wine
1 cup (8 fl oz) chicken stock

Preheat the oven to 160ºC (315ºF). Halve the chicken breasts and cut into pieces. Heat the oil in a frying pan over high heat. Add the chicken and cook for 1 minute each side or until golden. Place the chicken in a baking dish. Add the onions to the pan and cook for 4 minutes or until well browned. Spoon the onions, lemon, chillies, garlic, marjoram, wine and stock over the chicken. Cover the dish and bake for 20 minutes. Remove the cover and bake for a further 5 minutes.
To serve, place the chicken in bowls and serve with steamed couscous. Serves 4.
■ Available from delicatessens. Remove the flesh and rinse the rind well before slicing.

warm chicken salad

4 chicken breast fillets on the bone
2 green tomatoes, thickly sliced
1 tablespoon olive oil
cracked black pepper
250g (8 oz) baby rocket (arugula)
3 tablespoons coriander (cilantro) leaves
3 tablespoons mint leaves
1 cup sliced watermelon
dressing
1 tablespoon sesame oil
2 red chillies, chopped
1 tablespoon sesame seeds
3 tablespoons mirin* or sweet white wine
1 tablespoon light soy sauce
1 tablespoon lime juice

Cut the chicken into pieces. Brush the chicken and tomato slices with oil and sprinkle with pepper. Cook the chicken and tomatoes on a preheated hot barbecue or char grill (broiler) until tender and cooked through.
Arrange the rocket, coriander, mint and watermelon on plates and top with the chicken and tomatoes.
To make the dressing, place the oil in a saucepan over medium heat. Add the chillies and sesame seeds. Cook for 1 minute. Add the mirin, soy sauce and lime juice. Simmer for 1 minute. Pour the warm dressing over the salad and serve. Serves 4.

chicken, roast tomato and basil sandwiches

2 chicken breast fillets
6 roma tomatoes,* halved
olive oil
cracked black pepper
100g (3 1/4 oz) baby spinach leaves
1 cup basil leaves
3 tablespoons oil
8 slices sourdough or Turkish bread
100g (3 1/4 oz) aged cheddar cheese
lemon wedges

Preheat the oven to 160ºC (315ºF). Place the chicken and tomatoes in a baking dish and sprinkle with oil and pepper. Bake for 20 minutes or until the chicken is tender and cooked through. Shred the chicken.
Place the spinach, chicken, tomatoes and basil on half of the bread. Place the cheese on the remaining slices and grill (broil) under a hot grill (broiler) until the cheese is melted and is golden. Place the grilled cheese slices on top of the sandwiches and serve. Serves 4.

seafood

basics

The rules of cooking fish and seafood are simple: start with fresh produce, don't overcook it and serve it as soon as it is cooked. Easy.

fish fillets or cutlets

selection

A lot of fish are sold in fillet or cutlet form, which can make it hard to tell whether they are fresh. Fish fillets should look fresh and moist, and the flesh should be tight in texture and attached around the bones, if there are any. The fillets should be on ice and not sitting in water, and they should have no signs of discolouration or dryness.

storage

Wrap fish fillets in plastic wrap or store them in an airtight container. Most fish fillets and cutlets should keep for 2–3 days in the fridge. When taking your purchase home from the fishmonger, transport it in a cooler of some sort and refrigerate as soon as possible.

whole fish

selection

The easiest way to tell at a glance if a whole fish is fresh is by looking at its eyes. It should have full, bright, clear eyes. Fish that are a few days old often have cloudy, sunken eyes. The flesh should be firm and the scales should be tight. Ocean fish should have a pleasant sea smell. Freshwater fish should smell clean.

storage

Ask your fishmonger to gut and scale the fish, as this will extend its keeping life. Keep the fish cool while transporting it home. Store whole fish wrapped in plastic or in an airtight container for 2–3 days in the fridge.

shellfish

Shellfish can be divided into two groups: crustaceans and molluscs. Crustaceans (prawns/shrimp, lobsters and crabs) have an external skeleton that forms a shell. Molluscs (oysters, scallops, mussels, clams and octopuses) are invertebrates and are usually protected by a hard shell.

selection

Crustaceans should have an intact shell, no discolouration around the joints and a pleasant sea smell. Prawns should have no discolouration around the head. Whole lobsters and crabs should have a good heavy weight for their size. They should be on ice and not sitting in water. Molluscs such as oysters, mussels and pipis should be tightly closed in their shells, although pipis open and close regularly. It is easier to buy oysters that are already shucked or opened. They should be plump with a natural creamy colour and clear liquid. They should also be shiny and free from any shell pieces. Mussels sold as live should be tightly closed in their shells. If they are open, the mussel is dead. Scallops should have a creamy white-coloured meat, free from brown marking, with the roe intact. Small octopuses are the best for cooking. Look for firm flesh with a pleasant sea smell.

storage

Keep live crustaceans in a damp hessian bag in a cool place for 2 days. Prepared crustaceans should be wrapped in foil or stored in an airtight container for up to 2 days in the fridge. Keep live molluscs in a damp hessian bag in a cool place for up to 2 days. Clean octopuses before storing them in the fridge for up to 2 days. Shucked oysters should be kept on crushed ice in the fridge and covered with plastic wrap for up to 2 days. All other molluscs should be stored in an airtight container in the fridge for up to 2 days.

prawn

blue swimmer crab

garfish

oyster

scallop

garfish filled with sweet potato

seared tuna burgers with fried chilli salsa

lemon-fried yabbies with dill and potato cakes

garfish filled with sweet potato

12 garfish, gutted and backbone removed
plain (all-purpose) flour
olive oil for frying
filling
250g (8 oz) orange sweet potato (kumara)
2 tablespoons butter
¾ cup fresh breadcrumbs
1 tablespoon chopped preserved lemon■
1 teaspoon harissa*
1 teaspoon cinnamon
English spinach leaves, to serve

To make the filling, boil or steam the sweet potato until soft. Mash with the butter. Combine the mash, breadcrumbs, lemon, harissa and cinnamon. Spoon the filling into the cavities of the garfish and close securely with toothpicks. Toss the garfish lightly in flour and shallow-fry in hot oil for 1–2 minutes each side. Serve with English spinach. Serves 4.
■ Available from delicatessens. Remove the flesh and rinse the rind well before chopping.

seared tuna burgers with fried chilli salsa

4 x 120g (4 oz) tuna steaks
2 teaspoons kaffir lime* juice
1 tablespoon grated ginger
2 tablespoons soy sauce
4 poppyseed bagels, halved and toasted
salad greens
fried chilli salsa
1 tablespoon oil
4 green chillies, sliced
2 cloves garlic, sliced
4 green onions (scallions), chopped
1 green tomato, seeds removed and chopped
1 tablespoon brown sugar

Brush the tuna with the combined lime juice, ginger and soy sauce.
To make the chilli salsa, place the oil in a hot frying pan. Add the chillies and garlic and cook until the garlic is golden. Add the onions, tomato and sugar. Cook for a further 3 minutes. Remove the salsa from the heat and keep warm. Cook the tuna in a greased, hot frying pan or on a char grill (broiler) for no more than 45 seconds each side.
To serve, place the bagel bases on plates and top with the tuna steaks. Add the salad greens and top with the chilli salsa and bagel tops. Serves 4.

lemon-fried yabbies with dill and potato cakes

1 tablespoon oil
1 tablespoon butter
1 lemon, sliced
2 cloves garlic, sliced
12 yabbies (or small crayfish), halved and cleaned
2 tablespoons honey
cracked black pepper
dill and potato cakes
3 potatoes, peeled and grated
2 tablespoons chopped dill

To make the dill and potato cakes, combine the potatoes and dill in a small bowl. Place spoonfuls of the mixture on a greased barbecue plate or in a frying pan and flatten with a spatula. Cook for 3 minutes each side or until golden. Keep the cooked cakes warm on the coolest part of the barbecue while cooking the remaining mixture.
To cook the yabbies, heat the oil and butter in a frying pan or on a barbecue over medium heat. Add the lemon slices and garlic and cook for 4 minutes, stirring occasionally. Add the yabbies to the pan or barbecue. Drizzle with the honey and sprinkle with the pepper. Cook for 2–3 minutes or until the yabbies have changed colour and are cooked through. Serve with the dill and potato cakes. Serves 4.

tea-smoked baby salmon

4 baby salmon, gutted
2 limes, sliced
12 small sorrel* leaves
olive oil
cracked black pepper
3 tablespoons jasmine tea

Preheat the oven to 180°C (350°F). Place the salmon in a baking dish. Fill the cavities with lime slices and sorrel. Sprinkle the fish with oil and pepper and bake for 25 minutes or until cooked through. Drain the salmon on paper towel.
Place the tea in the bottom of a large wok. Heat until the tea starts to smoke. Place the salmon on a rack in the wok and cover with a lid.
Allow the salmon to smoke for 10 minutes. (This is best done in a well-ventilated kitchen.)
Serve the salmon warm or cold with a salad of greens and whole-egg mayonnaise mixed with lime and pepper. Serves 4.

tea-smoked baby salmon

garlic-baked blue eye cod

wok-fried salted chilli crab

garlic-baked blue eye cod

6 roma tomatoes,* halved
4 blue eye cod cutlets
4 cloves garlic, sliced
1 tablespoon lemon thyme leaves
pepper
baby English spinach leaves
lime wedges

Preheat the oven to 180°C (350°F). Place the tomatoes on a baking tray lined with non-stick baking paper. Bake for 25 minutes or until soft and lightly browned.
Place the blue eye cod cutlets on a baking tray lined with non-stick baking paper and sprinkle with the garlic, lemon thyme and pepper. Place in the oven with the tomatoes and bake for 10–15 minutes or until cooked.
Serve the blue eye cod on a bed of baby spinach leaves with the tomatoes and lime wedges. Serves 4.

wok-fried salted chilli crab

3 green (uncooked) crabs
2 tablespoons oil
2 red chillies, chopped
1 tablespoon sea salt
1 tablespoon cracked black pepper
lime wedges

Remove the limbs and claws from the crabs. Cut the body portions in half and clean well. Crack the claws with the back of a knife or cleaver. Heat a wok or frying pan over high heat. Add the oil, chillies, salt and pepper and cook for 1 minute. Add the crab pieces and stir-fry for 5–7 minutes or until the shells change colour and the flesh is white and tender.
Serve the crabs with lime wedges and eat with your fingers. The spices on the shell will flavour the crab meat. Serves 4.
Note: If the crab claws are large, lightly steam them before adding them to the spices in the wok.

wok-steamed scallops with broth

24 scallops
3 tablespoons shredded ginger
3 tablespoons coriander (cilantro) leaves
1½ cups (12 fl oz) water
1 stalk lemon grass,* bruised
2 kaffir lime* leaves
2 tablespoons miso*
2 tablespoons oil
⅓ cup Thai basil* leaves

Remove any brown from the scallops and sprinkle over the ginger and coriander. Pour the water into a wok or frying pan and add the lemon grass, lime leaves and scallops. Cover, place the wok over medium heat and allow the scallops to steam for 3–5 minutes or until cooked.
Remove the scallops, keeping any excess cooking juices in the wok. Cover the scallops and set aside. Add enough water to the wok to make about 4 cups (32 fl oz) of liquid. Add the miso and stir to dissolve. Allow the liquid to simmer for 2 minutes.
Heat the oil in a frying pan over medium heat. Add the Thai basil, fry until crisp and drain on paper towel.
To serve, place the scallops on plates, top with the fried Thai basil and drizzle over a little of the cooking oil. Serve with small bowls of the broth. Serves 4.

wok-steamed scallops with broth

Asian-style infused swordfish with greens

bay and chervil fried salmon steaks   crispy spiced snapper

Asian-style infused swordfish with greens

300g (9½ oz) assorted Asian greens (for example, bok choy*,
  choy sum*, snow pea (mange tout) shoots)
4 swordfish steaks
4 stems coriander (cilantro)
8 kaffir lime* leaves
4 stalks lemon grass,* halved
4 green chillies, sliced
cracked black pepper and lime wedges to serve

Line 4 bamboo steamers* with 4 large pieces of non-stick baking paper, allowing a generous overhang. Place the mixed greens in the base of the steamers. Wrap a coriander stem around each swordfish steak and place on the greens. Top the swordfish steaks with the kaffir lime leaves, lemon grass and chillies. Fold over the baking paper to cover the fish. Cover each steamer with its lid. Place the steamers over simmering water and steam for 4–5 minutes or until the fish is cooked. Serve with pepper and lime wedges and bowls of steamed rice. Serves 4.

bay and chervil fried salmon steaks

1 tablespoon olive oil
2 teaspoons sea salt
500g (1 lb) orange sweet potatoes (kumara), peeled
  and chopped
350g (11¼ oz) parsnips, peeled and chopped
60g (2 oz) butter
2 tablespoons oil
8 bay leaves
3 tablespoons chopped chervil
1 teaspoon cracked black pepper
2 pieces lime rind
4 x 185g (6 oz) salmon steaks
125g (4 oz) baby English spinach leaves

Preheat the oven to 200°C (400°F). Place the olive oil, salt, sweet potatoes and parsnips in a baking dish and shake to combine. Bake in the oven for 35 minutes or until crisp and golden. Place the butter and oil in a frying pan over medium heat. Add the bay leaves, chervil, pepper and lime rind and cook for 2 minutes. Add the salmon steaks and cook for 1–2 minutes on each side or until cooked medium rare.
To serve, place the sweet potatoes and parsnips on plates. Top with the baby spinach and salmon. Spoon the pan juices over the fish. Serves 4.

crispy spiced snapper

2 teaspoons ground cumin
1 green chilli
3 stems coriander (cilantro)
2 cloves garlic
2 slices ginger
2 teaspoons garam masala
4 small snapper, gutted
oil for deep-frying

Place the cumin, chilli, coriander, garlic, ginger and garam masala in a small food processor or mortar and pestle and process or pound until smooth.
Make deep slits in the flesh of the snapper. Rub the herb mixture over the fish and allow to marinate in the fridge for 1 hour.
To cook, deep-fry the snapper in hot oil for 1–2 minutes or until crisp and cooked through. This is most easily done in a wok. Serve with thin fried potato crisps. Serves 4.

lime prawns with green mango salad

16 large green (raw) prawns (shrimp)
2 tablespoons grated lime rind
3 tablespoons lime juice
2 red chillies, finely chopped
2 teaspoons cumin seeds
2 teaspoons sesame oil
green mango salad
2 green mangoes, peeled
4 green onions (scallions), chopped
2 red chillies, sliced
2 tablespoons brown sugar
2 tablespoons lime juice
½ cup mint leaves
¼ cup coriander (cilantro) leaves

Peel the prawn bodies, leaving the heads and tails intact. Thread onto bamboo skewers. Combine the lime rind, lime juice, chillies, cumin seeds and sesame oil. Brush thoroughly over the prawns and allow to stand for 10 minutes.
To make the green mango salad, finely slice the mangoes and combine with the onions, chillies, sugar, lime juice, mint and coriander. Place the salad in small piles on plates. Cook the prawns on a hot char grill (broiler) or barbecue for 1 minute each side or until cooked through. To serve, place the prawns on the green mango salad. Serves 4.

lime prawns with green mango salad

fruit

basics

seasons

The best time to buy fruit is at the peak of its season, when it has optimum flavour, texture and colour. As an added bonus, its price is at its lowest when it's in season.

storage

In the warmer months it's best to keep fruit in the fridge, with the exception of bananas. (Their skins turn black but the flesh remains fine.) The fruit and vegetable compartments are the best place for fruit in the fridge. Berries should be placed in a bowl lined with absorbent paper and stored in the fridge. Fruit that needs to be ripened should be stored at room temperature and stored in the fridge when it's ripe. If fruit is cut, wrap it well in plastic wrap and store it in the fridge. Many people believe that fruit should not be eaten straight from the fridge, that its flavour is better when it's close to room temperature. I tend to disagree. I think there is nothing better than a cold peach or mango on a hot summer day.

selection

Purchase fruit in season that is firm and of good colour, without blemishes or bruises. To choose melons, tap them with the heel of your hand. They should sound full. Rockmelons and honeydew melons are easily tested for ripeness by their smell at the stalk end. The ends should be firm with a little movement. Apples should be firm with undamaged skin. Pears ripen from the inside out, so choose firm, plump pears with undamaged skin. Stone fruits should be firm with undamaged skin, which should be bright, not dull and wilted. Citrus fruits should be heavy for their size and have undamaged, glossy skin. Figs should be soft and plump with a sweet smell. Figs with a slightly sour smell are over-ripe. Grapes should have fresh green stalks and plump fruit. Avoid grapes with split skins. Green grapes are ripe when they have a yellowish tinge and dark grapes are ripe when they have no green tinge. Nashi should have good weight for their size, which indicates they are full of juice. Mangoes should have smooth, unblemished, firm skin with a wonderful smell.

preparation

Some fruit, such as bananas and apples, brown when cut and the flesh is exposed to the air. To avoid browning, brush the cut surfaces with a little lemon juice. For nutritional reasons, peel fruit only if necessary. Wash fruit well under cold running water before preparing.

apricots

nectarine

peach

plums

raspberries

blueberries

strawberry

apricots in sauternes syrup

almond peach galette

lime and raspberry tart

apricots in sauternes syrup

12 apricots
1/4 cup sugar
1/3 cup (23/4 fl oz) water
11/2 cups (12 fl oz) sauternes or sweet dessert wine
1 vanilla bean*

Place the apricots in a bowl of boiling water and allow to stand for 4 minutes. Drain the water and peel the apricots. Place the sugar and water in a saucepan over low heat and cook, stirring, until the sugar is dissolved. Bring the syrup to a simmer and add the sauternes and vanilla bean. Simmer for 5 minutes. Add the apricots and simmer for 3–5 minutes or until soft.
Serve in a deep plate with honey biscuits (see page 152). Serves 4.

almond peach galette

4 peaches
185g (6 oz) ready-prepared puff pastry
1/2 cup ground almonds
2 tablespoons soft butter
1/2 teaspoon vanilla extract
4 tablespoons demerara sugar*

Preheat the oven to 200°C (400°F). Cut the peaches in half, remove the stones and slice the flesh.
Cut the pastry into 4 rectangles.
Combine the almonds, butter and vanilla and spread the mixture down the centre of the pastry. Top the pastry with the peaches and sprinkle with the sugar. Place the galette on a baking tray and bake for 15 minutes or until the pastry is puffed and golden.
Serve with thick cream or ice cream. Serves 4.

lime and raspberry tart

2 quantities or 500 g (1 lb 2 oz) sweet shortcrust pastry*
300g (10 oz) raspberries
icing (confectioner's) sugar
filling
1/2 cup (4 fl oz) lime juice
11/2 cups (12 fl oz) cream
1/2 cup (4 fl oz) coconut cream
2/3 cup caster (superfine) sugar
4 eggs, lightly beaten

Preheat the oven to 150°C (300°F). Roll out the pastry until 3mm (1/8 inch) thick. Place in a deep 23cm (9 inch) round tart tin and refrigerate for 30 minutes. Line the pastry shell with non-stick baking paper and fill with baking weights or rice. Bake for 5 minutes. Remove the weights and paper. Bake for a further 5 minutes.
To make the filling, combine the lime juice, cream, coconut cream, sugar and eggs. Pour into the pastry base and cook for 30 minutes or until just set. Refrigerate the tart until cold. To serve, top with the raspberries and dust with icing sugar. Serves 6 to 8.

nectarine ice cream

4 nectarines, stones removed
2 tablespoons lime juice
2 cups (16 fl oz) cream (pouring or single)
1 cup (8 fl oz) milk
6 egg yolks
2/3 cup sugar

Process the nectarines and lime juice in a food processor or blender until smooth. Push the puree through a sieve. (You should have 1 cup (8 fl oz) of sieved nectarine puree.) Place the cream, egg yolks and sugar in a saucepan over low heat and stir for 10 minutes or until the mixture has thickened slightly. Allow to cool.
Stir the nectarine puree through the cream mixture. Pour into an ice-cream maker and follow the manufacturer's instructions until the ice cream is firm and frozen. Alternatively, pour the mixture into a metal container and freeze for 1 hour. Remove from the freezer and beat until smooth. Return to the freezer for 30 minutes. Remove from the freezer again, beat the mixture and then return it to the freezer until firm. Serves 6.

nectarine ice cream

fruit

nashi with lime and ginger   simple apple tart

honey biscuits with mixed berries   fresh plum cake

nashi with lime and ginger

1 cup sugar
4 cups (32 fl oz) water
5cm (2 inch) piece ginger, shredded
3 tablespoons lime juice
rind of 1 lime, cut into thin strips
4 nashi

Place the sugar, water, ginger, lime juice and rind in a saucepan and stir over low heat until the sugar is dissolved. Increase the heat and allow the mixture to simmer for 5 minutes.
Peel and halve the nashi. Brush with some extra lime juice to prevent browning. Place in a bowl and pour over the syrup. Refrigerate for 2 hours, stirring occasionally. Serve with the lime and ginger syrup and a scoop of toasted coconut ice cream. Serves 4.

simple apple tart

2 green apples, peeled, cored and chopped
2 tablespoons water
2 teaspoons grated lemon rind
2 tablespoons sugar
250g (8 oz) ready-prepared puff pastry
3 green apples, extra
25g (1 oz) butter, melted
1 tablespoon sugar, extra

Place the apples, water, lemon rind and sugar in a saucepan. Cover and cook over medium heat until the apples are very soft. Mash with a fork until almost smooth. Allow to cool.
Preheat the oven to 180°C (350°F). Roll out the pastry on a lightly floured surface into an 18 x 28cm (7 x 11 inch) rectangle. Spread with the apple puree, leaving a 3cm (1 1/4 inch) border. Peel, core and thinly slice the extra apples. Arrange on top of the apple puree. Brush with butter and sprinkle with the extra sugar. Place on a baking tray and bake for 30 minutes or until the pastry is puffed and golden. Serve slices with scoops of vanilla bean ice cream (see page 174) or thick cream. Serves 8.

honey biscuits with mixed berries

1/4 cup caster (superfine) sugar
2 tablespoons honey
1/2 cup plain (all-purpose) flour
1 egg white
45g (1 1/2 oz) butter, melted

filling
3/4 cup (6 fl oz) thick cream
2 tablespoons pure icing (confectioner's) sugar
2 teaspoons grated lime rind
500–600g (1–1 1/4 lb) mixed berries

Preheat the oven to 180°C (350°F). To make the biscuits, place the sugar, honey, flour, egg white and butter in a bowl and stir until smooth. Drop spoonfuls of the mixture onto greased baking trays. Bake for 8–10 minutes or until the biscuits are a dark golden colour. Cool on wire racks until they are crisp.
To make the filling, mix together the cream, icing sugar and lime rind.
To serve, place a honey biscuit on a plate and top with a spoonful of cream mixture and some berries. Top with another honey biscuit and sprinkle with icing sugar. Serves 6 to 8.

fresh plum cake

4 blood plums, seeded and chopped
155g (5 oz) butter
3/4 cup caster (superfine) sugar
3 eggs
1 1/2 cups ground hazelnuts or almonds
1 teaspoon vanilla extract
1 1/2 cups self-raising flour*
1/2 teaspoon baking powder

Preheat the oven to 180°C (350°F). Process the plums in a food processor or blender until smooth. Set aside. Place the butter and sugar in a bowl and beat until light and creamy. Add the eggs and beat well.
Stir the plums, hazelnuts, vanilla, flour and baking powder through the egg mixture and pour into a greased 20cm (8 inch) cake tin. Bake for 45–55 minutes or until the cake is cooked when tested with a skewer. Allow the cake to stand in the tin for 5 minutes. Serve hot with thick cream and extra slices of blood plum. Serves 8 to 10.

sugar-grilled figs

6 fresh figs, halved
2 tablespoons dessert wine
1/2 cup brown sugar
60g (2 oz) butter, chopped
toffee ice cream to serve

Place the figs on a grill (broiler) tray, flesh-side up. Brush with the dessert wine and sprinkle with the sugar and butter. Place under a hot grill for 2–3 minutes or until the figs are golden. Serve with toffee ice cream. Serves 4 to 6.

sugar-grilled figs

butter & baking

basics

sifting

Sift flours and lumpy sugars to incorporate air into them and to remove lumps that may not break down when mixing.

flours

Flours come in a wide variety, including white, wholemeal, plain (all-purpose) and self-raising. Wholemeal flour gives finished products a heavier texture and a wheatier flavour. Self-raising flour is 1 cup plain flour with 1 teaspoon baking powder added.

whisking

Whisking can be done with a hand wire whisk or with the electric whisk attachment on electric mixers. Whisking breaks up ingredients so they combine. It also aerates ingredients such as eggs.

folding

When folding, use a metal spoon to cut through ingredients and fold them over each other, being careful not to stir the air out of the mixture.

creaming

When creaming butter and sugar, the butter should be cold but softened slightly. Melted or partially melted butter will change the texture and rising of the end result. Cream butter and sugar until the mixture becomes a pale creamy colour and looks light and aerated. It's possible to overcream the mixture, so don't overbeat.

beating

Beating can be done by hand with a wooden spoon or with an electric mixer, depending on the instructions in the recipe. Beating ingredients will combine and aerate them. When beating, run a plastic or rubber scraper down the sides of the bowl so ingredients are well combined. Using a food processor to beat will not aerate the ingredients; it will just make them smooth. When beating egg whites, make sure the bowl and beaters are clean and dry for maximum volume. When beating cream, make sure it is well chilled. If it is a hot day, chill the bowl and the beaters as well.

butters

Butters can be salted and unsalted. When baking with delicate flavours, unsalted butter is better. For nutty-tasting butter for friands, melt butter over low heat, remove from heat before it is all melted and stir. For some savoury sauces, heat the butter and allow it to slowly simmer until it has turned a light golden colour. When creaming butter, remove it from the fridge a few hours before you need it and use at room temperature. When making pastry, butter must be cold and firm to ensure the pastry has a fine, crisp crumb.

sugars

White sugar, or granulated table sugar, is the most common type of sugar and is used extensively. White sugar is processed to medium-sized crystals. Caster (superfine) sugar has finer, smaller crystals than white sugar. It dissolves faster than white sugar and is often used in meringues and cakes. Icing (confectioner's) sugar has been ground to a powder. It can be purchased as pure icing sugar or icing sugar mixture, which has cornflour and/or calcium phosphate added to prevent it from caking while being stored. Dark brown sugar, brown sugar and light brown sugar are soft moist sugars with very small crystals. They have a distinctive flavour from the molasses coating each crystal. Brown sugars are great for puddings and baking. Demerara sugar has been treated with light brown molasses, which gives it a toffee taste. Demerara sugar is also great for baking.

creaming

whisking

cup measures

spoon measures

sifting

pound cake

375g (12 oz) butter
1½ cups sugar
1 teaspoon vanilla extract
6 eggs

3 cups plain (all-purpose) flour
1 tablespoon baking powder
2 tablespoons milk

STEP ONE
Preheat the oven to
160°C (315°F). Place
the butter and sugar in
a bowl and beat until
light and creamy.

STEP TWO
Add the vanilla and
eggs, one at a time,
and beat well.

STEP THREE
Sift together the flour
and baking powder.
Fold with the milk into
the butter and eggs.

STEP FOUR
Pour the batter
into a 20cm (8 inch)
greased square
cake tin. Bake for
1 hour 10 minutes
or until the cake is
cooked when tested
with a skewer.

variations

ORANGE POUND CAKE
Add 3 tablespoons finely grated orange
rind to the butter mixture.

LEMON POUND CAKE
Add 2 tablespoons finely grated lemon
rind to the butter mixture.

COCONUT POUND CAKE
Add 1 cup desiccated coconut when folding
the flour through the butter and eggs.

POPPYSEED POUND CAKE
Add 3 tablespoons poppyseeds when
folding in the flour.

pound cake

blueberry and lemon friands

175g (5¾ oz) unsalted butter
1 cup almond meal
1 tablespoon finely grated lemon rind
1⅔ cups icing (confectioner's) sugar, sifted
5 tablespoons plain (all-purpose) flour, sifted
5 egg whites
200g (6½ oz) blueberries, frozen or fresh

Preheat the oven to 200°C (400°F). Place the butter in
a saucepan over low heat and cook until a very light
golden colour.
Place the almond meal, lemon rind, icing sugar and flour
in a bowl and mix to combine. Add the egg whites and
mix. Add the melted butter and mix until combined.
Pour the mixture into greased ½-cup friand, muffin or patty
tins. Sprinkle with the blueberries and bake for 15 minutes
or until golden and springy to touch. Cool the friands
on wire racks and dust with extra icing sugar to serve.
Makes 10 to 12.

caramel puddings

125g (4 oz) butter
1⅓ cups brown sugar
4 eggs, separated
¾ cup self-raising flour*
½ cup (4 fl oz) milk
caramel sauce
½ cup brown sugar
2 tablespoons water
60g (2 oz) butter
⅓ cup (2¾ fl oz) cream (single or pouring)

Preheat the oven to 180°C (350°F). Place the butter and
sugar in a bowl and beat until light and creamy. Add the
egg yolks and beat well. Stir the flour and milk through.
Place the egg whites in a separate bowl and beat until soft
peaks form. Fold gently into the butter mixture and spoon
into six 1-cup capacity ramekins.* Place the ramekins in a
baking dish and fill the dish with enough water to come
halfway up the sides of the ramekins. Bake for 20 minutes
or until the puddings are puffed and golden.
While the puddings are cooking, make the caramel sauce.
Place the sugar, water and butter in a saucepan and stir
over low heat until the sugar is melted. Add the cream and
allow the sauce to simmer for 5 minutes or until thickened.
To serve, place the ramekins on plates and top the
puddings with some caramel sauce. Serves 6.

chocolate cake with glaze

300g (10 oz) dark chocolate, chopped
250g (8 oz) butter
5 eggs
4 tablespoons sugar
½ cup ground almonds
1 cup self-raising flour,* sifted
chocolate glaze
½ cup (4 fl oz) cream
125g (4 oz) dark chocolate, chopped

Preheat the oven to 160°C (315°F). Place the chocolate
and butter in a saucepan over low heat and stir until
smooth. Set aside. Place the eggs and sugar in a bowl
and beat until light and fluffy (about 6 minutes). Fold the
almonds, flour and chocolate mixture through the eggs
and sugar. Grease and line a 23 cm (9 inch) round cake tin
with non-stick baking paper. Pour in the mixture and bake
for 45 minutes or until the cake is cooked when tested with
a skewer. Cool the cake in the tin.
To make the chocolate glaze, heat the cream in a saucepan
until almost boiling. Remove the pan from the heat. Stir
in the chocolate and continue stirring until smooth.
Spread the cake with the chocolate glaze. Cut the cake
into wedges and serve with chilled mixed berries and thick
cream. Serves 8 to 10.

patty cakes

1½ cups self-raising flour*
⅔ cup caster (superfine) sugar
155g (5 oz) butter
3 eggs, lightly beaten
¼ cup (2 fl oz) milk
1 teaspoon vanilla extract
whipped cream or lemon curd

Preheat the oven to 180°C (350°F). Place the flour, sugar,
butter, eggs, milk and vanilla in a bowl and beat until
well mixed. Continue to beat until the mixture is light
and creamy. Spoon the mixture into patty-cake cases
in tins until the cases are three-quarters full. Bake for
20 minutes or until the cakes are golden and cooked
when tested with a skewer. Allow to cool on wire racks.
To serve, remove a round of cake using a teaspoon and
fill the hole with whipped cream or lemon curd.
Top the filling with the removed piece of cake and sprinkle
with icing (confectioner's) sugar. Serve at a grown-ups'
afternoon tea party. Makes 24.

blueberry and lemon friands

chocolate cake with glaze

caramel pudding

patty cakes

vanilla sugar cookies

almond shortbread

chocolate chip cookie

chocolate brownie

vanilla sugar cookies

185g (6 oz) butter
1 cup caster (superfine) sugar
1½ teaspoons vanilla extract
2½ cups plain (all-purpose) flour
1 egg

Preheat the oven to 180°C (350°F). Process the butter, sugar and vanilla in a food processor until smooth. Add the flour and egg. Process until a smooth dough forms. Knead the dough lightly, wrap in plastic wrap and refrigerate for 30 minutes.
Roll out the dough on sheets of non-stick baking paper until approximately 5mm (¼ inch) thick. Cut the dough into the desired shapes using cookie cutters and place on baking trays. Bake for 10–12 minutes or until light golden. Cool the cookies on racks. Makes approximately 30 cookies.

almond shortbread

250g (8 oz) butter
¾ cup icing (confectioner's) sugar
1 teaspoon vanilla extract
2 cups plain (all-purpose) flour
100g (3¼ oz) toasted blanched almonds, chopped
extra icing (confectioner's) sugar for dusting

Preheat the oven to 160°C (315°F). Place the butter, sugar and vanilla in a bowl and beat until light and creamy. Add the flour and almonds and mix to form a smooth dough. Refrigerate for 5 minutes or until the dough is firm.
Take 2 tablespoons of dough at a time and roll into crescents. Place the crescents on baking trays lined with non-stick paper and bake for 15 minutes or until the shortbread is golden.
Cool on wire racks and sprinkle liberally with icing sugar. Makes 20.

chocolate chip cookies

125g (4 oz) butter, softened
½ teaspoon vanilla extract
1 cup brown sugar
1 egg
1 cup plain (all-purpose) flour
1 cup self-raising flour*
1 cup desiccated coconut
250g (8 oz) chopped chocolate

Preheat the oven to 190°C (375°F). Place the butter, vanilla extract and sugar in a bowl and beat until creamy. Add the egg and beat. Stir through the flours, coconut and chocolate. Roll 2 tablespoons of mixture at a time into balls. Place the balls on baking trays lined with non-stick baking paper and flatten slightly. Bake for 15 minutes or until the cookies are lightly browned. Cool on trays. Serve with hot chocolate. Makes 20.

chocolate brownies

125g (4 oz) butter
125g (4 oz) dark chocolate
2 eggs
1 cup caster (superfine) sugar
1 cup plain (all-purpose) flour
2 tablespoons self-raising flour*
¾ cup chopped pecan or macadamia nuts

Preheat the oven to 180°C (350°F). Place the butter and chocolate in a saucepan over very low heat and stir until just smooth.
Place the eggs and sugar in a bowl and beat until pale and thick. Fold the chocolate mixture, sifted flours and nuts through the sugar and eggs. Pour the mixture into a greased 20cm (8 inch) square cake tin. Bake for 30 minutes or until set. Allow to cool and cut into squares.
Serve with strong espresso coffee. Makes 12 squares.

steamed coconut puddings with lime

orange semolina cake

banana maple syrup muffin

steamed coconut puddings with lime

175g (5¾ oz) unsalted butter
85g (2¾ oz) caster (superfine) sugar
1 teaspoon vanilla extract
3 eggs, lightly beaten
1 cup self-raising flour*, sifted
100g (3¼ oz) desiccated coconut
lime syrup
½ cup sugar
1 cup (8 fl oz) water
3 tablespoons lime juice
rind of 2 limes, shredded
3 cardamom pods, bruised

Place the butter, sugar and vanilla in a bowl and beat until light and creamy. Add the eggs and beat well. Fold in the flour and coconut. Pour the mixture into six ¾-cup capacity, well-greased ramekins.*
Cover the mixture with small circles of greased paper. Place the ramekins in a steamer. Steam the puddings over rapidly simmering water for 30 minutes or until they are cooked when tested with a skewer.
To make the syrup, place the sugar, water, lime juice and rind, and cardamom pods in a saucepan and stir over low heat until the sugar is dissolved. Allow the syrup to simmer for 3–5 minutes or until it has thickened slightly. Invert the puddings onto plates and pour over the lime syrup. Serve with thick cream. Serves 6.

orange semolina cake

⅔ cup plain (all-purpose) flour
½ teaspoon baking powder
2 cups fine semolina
4 eggs, separated
¾ cup caster (superfine) sugar
½ cup (4 fl oz) olive oil
1 tablespoon grated orange rind
½ cup (4 fl oz) orange juice
syrup
1½ cups caster (superfine) sugar
1¼ cups (6 fl oz) orange juice
1½ tablespoons grated orange rind

Preheat the oven to 180°C (350°F). Place the flour, baking powder and semolina in a bowl and mix to combine. Place the egg yolks, sugar, oil and orange rind in a bowl and beat until well combined. Fold the egg yolk mixture into the flour mixture with the orange juice.
Place the egg whites in a bowl and beat until soft peaks form. Fold into the flour and egg yolk mixture. Pour into a greased 20cm (8 inch) square cake tin. Bake for 45 minutes or until the cake is cooked when tested with a skewer. While the cake is cooking, prepare the syrup. Place the sugar, orange juice and rind in a saucepan over low heat and stir until the sugar is dissolved. Allow to simmer for 3 minutes. Pour half of the syrup over the cake.
To serve, cut the cake into wedges and spoon over the remaining syrup. Serve with thick cream. Serves 6 to 8.

banana maple syrup muffins

2 cups self-raising flour*
½ teaspoon ground cinnamon
½ cup sugar
300g (10 oz) sour cream
1 egg
3 tablespoons maple syrup
3 tablespoons vegetable oil
3 bananas, chopped

Preheat the oven to 200°C (400°F). Place the flour, cinnamon and sugar in a bowl and mix to combine. Place the sour cream, egg, maple syrup, oil and bananas in a bowl and whisk to combine. Add the banana mixture to the dry ingredients and mix until just combined.
Spoon the mixture into greased ½-cup capacity muffin tins. Bake for 25–30 minutes or until the muffins are cooked when tested with a skewer.
Serve with extra maple syrup. Makes 12.

12

milk & cream

basics

sour cream

Sour cream is cream with a culture added, which slightly sours and thickens the cream. Sour cream is often used in cheesecakes, cakes, sauces and soups. Sour cream makes a great topping for baked potatoes and is a quick accompaniment for many savoury dishes.

buttermilk

Originally, buttermilk was the liquid that remained after making butter from cream, hence its name. It is now made from skim (reduced-fat) milk and cultures. It has a slightly acidic taste and a thick consistency. Buttermilk not only adds flavour to cooking, its acid content also reacts with raising agents, giving some baked and flour products a lighter texture.

cream

Cream comes in a variety of forms from single, or pouring, cream to thickened cream, which has gelatine added. Gelatine helps the cream hold its shape when whipped. Cream should be well chilled before whipping. Cream also comes as thick, or double, cream, which has a higher butterfat content, making it easy to spoon and dollop. Clotted cream has been heated to just below boiling point, and then cooled. It is thick and has a rich nutty flavour and, often, a yellowish crust. Serve clotted cream with cakes, fruits and puddings.

coconut cream

Coconut cream is the extract from the first pressing of the grated flesh of mature coconuts. Subsequent pressings make coconut milk. Coconut cream is a thick greyish-white milk, which is used in sweets or curries. It will curdle if boiled. To prevent curdling, gently simmer coconut cream or add a paste of cornflour (cornstarch) and water if it is to be well heated.

milk

Cows' milk is the most readily available form of milk. It is usually sold in homogenised form, which means the cream is evenly distributed through the milk. It is also pasteurised, which means it has been heat-treated to kill any bacteria that could spoil the milk. Pasteurisation also gives the milk a longer shelf life.

yoghurt

Yoghurt is made by warming milk and adding a culture of safe bacteria that thickens the milk to a smooth, spoonable consistency. Yoghurt has a fresh, tangy taste. It can be made with cows', sheep's, or goats' milk. Yoghurt makes a good substitute for sour cream.

cream

milk

yoghurt

coconut cream

sour cream

buttermilk

crème brûlée

2 cups (16 fl oz) cream (single
   or pouring)
1 vanilla bean*
5 egg yolks
3 tablespoons caster (superfine) sugar
1/3 cup sugar

variations

CINNAMON BRULEE
Add 2 cinnamon sticks to cream when
infusing vanilla. Remove cinnamon
after infusion.

LIME AND COCONUT BRULEE
Add 4 large pieces of lime rind and
1/3 cup shredded coconut to cream
when infusing vanilla. Strain cream
through a fine sieve after infusing.

LEMON AND BAY LEAF BRULEE
Add 4 pieces of lemon rind and 3 bay
leaves to cream when infusing vanilla.
Remove lemon rind and bay leaves
after infusion.

STEP ONE
Place the cream and vanilla bean in a
saucepan over low heat. Allow the
cream to simmer for 3 minutes. Remove
from the heat and allow to stand for
20 minutes for the vanilla flavour to
infuse into the cream.

STEP TWO
Preheat the oven to 180°C (350°F). Add
the egg yolks and caster sugar to the
cream and stir over low heat until the
mixture thickens enough to coat the
back of a spoon. Remove the vanilla
bean from the custard.

STEP THREE
Pour the mixture into four 1/2-cup
capacity ramekins.* Place the ramekins
in a baking dish and fill the baking dish
with enough water to come halfway up
the sides of the ramekins. Place the dish
in the oven and bake for 20 minutes or
until the custards are just set.

STEP FOUR
Remove the ramekins from the baking
dish and refrigerate for 1 hour or until
they are cold. Place the ramekins in a
tray and sprinkle the tops with sugar.
Put ice cubes in the tray around the
ramekins and place the tray under a
preheated hot grill (broiler) for 1 minute
or until the sugar melts and is golden.
Serves 4.

crème brûlées

peaches and berries in baked cream

4 eggs
1/3 cup sugar
1 1/3 cups (10 3/4 fl oz) cream
1 teaspoon vanilla extract
3 tablespoons plain (all-purpose) flour
2 peaches, sliced
1 cup mixed berries

Preheat the oven to 160ºC (315ºF). Place the eggs, sugar, cream and vanilla in a bowl and beat until frothy. Sift the flour over the egg mixture and whisk until smooth. Pour 3/4 cup of the cream mixture into a greased 23cm (9 inch) pie dish. Bake for 5 minutes or until the cream is just set. Remove the dish from the oven and sprinkle the peaches and berries over the baked cream. Pour the remaining cream mixture over the fruit and bake for 15–20 minutes or until set. Serve in wedges with ice cream. Serves 6.

vanilla bean ice cream

2 cups (16 fl oz) cream (single or pouring)
1 cup (8 fl oz) milk
2 vanilla beans,* split
8 egg yolks
2/3 cup caster (superfine) sugar
1 teaspoon vanilla extract

Place the cream, milk and vanilla beans in a saucepan over low heat. Allow to heat for 4 minutes. Remove the pan from the heat and allow to stand for 30 minutes. Add the egg yolks and sugar to the cream mixture and stir over low heat until the mixture thickens slightly. (It should coat the back of a wooden spoon.) Remove the vanilla beans and stir the vanilla extract through the cream mixture.
Pour the mixture into an ice-cream machine and freeze according to the manufacturer's instructions. Alternatively, pour the mixture into a metal container and freeze for 1 hour. Beat the mixture to break up the ice crystals and refreeze for 3 hours or until the ice cream has set and is firm.
Serve in chilled bowls with cookies or biscotti. Serves 6.

strawberry ice-cream sandwiches

16 caramel waffles
ice cream
2 1/2 cups (20 fl oz) cream (single or pouring)
3 egg yolks
1/3 cup caster (superfine) sugar
3/4 cup pureed strawberries

To make the ice cream, place the cream, egg yolks and sugar in a saucepan and stir over low heat for 5 minutes or until the mixture coats the back of a spoon. Allow the mixture to cool.
Add the strawberries to the cream mixture and place in an ice-cream machine and freeze according to the manufacturer's instructions. Alternatively, pour the mixture into a metal container and freeze for 1 hour. Beat the mixture to break up the ice crystals and refreeze for 3 hours or until the ice cream has set and is firm.
Spread the ice cream over a wafer and sandwich together with another wafer. Refreeze or serve immediately. Serves 8.

baked raspberry cheesecake

125g (4 oz) plain sweet biscuits, crushed
125g (4 oz) ground almonds
125g (4 oz) butter, melted
filling
250g (8 oz) cream cheese, softened
250g (8 oz) ricotta cheese
3 eggs
1 cup sugar
1 cup (8 fl oz) sour cream
1 tablespoon grated lemon rind
3 tablespoons lemon juice
1 tablespoon cornflour (cornstarch) blended with
  1 tablespoon water
250g (8 oz) raspberries

Combine the biscuits, almonds and butter. Press into the base of a greased 20cm (8 inch) springform cake tin. Refrigerate.
Preheat the oven to 150°C (300°F). To make the filling, process the cream cheese, ricotta, eggs, sugar, sour cream, lemon rind and juice, and cornflour mixture in a food processor until smooth. (Alternatively, beat with an electric mixer until the filling is smooth.) Pour the mixture over the base and sprinkle with the raspberries. Bake for 40 minutes or until the cheesecake is just set. Refrigerate until the cheesecake is cold and firm.
Cut into wedges and serve with thick cream if desired. Serves 8.

peaches and berries in baked cream

vanilla bean ice cream   strawberry ice cream sandwiches

baked raspberry cheesecake

passionfruit curd tart brûlée

passionfruit curd
tart brûlée

1 quantity or 250g (8 oz) sweet shortcrust pastry*
passionfruit curd filling
1 cup caster (superfine) sugar
4 eggs
1 cup (8 fl oz) cream (single or pouring)
200ml (7 fl oz) passionfruit pulp
2 tablespoons lemon juice
sugar for sprinkling

Preheat the oven to 180°C (350°F). Roll out the pastry to
fit a 25cm (10 inch) removable-base tart tin. Prick a few
holes in the pastry and place a piece of baking paper in
the pastry shell. Fill the shell with baking weights or rice.
Bake for 10 minutes. Remove the weights and paper. Bake
the shell for a further 5 minutes. (This process is called
blind baking and will keep the tart shell crisp when it has
a wet filling.)
To make the filling, place the sugar, eggs, cream,
passionfruit pulp and lemon juice in a bowl. Whisk to
combine. Pour the filling into the tart shell and bake for
30 minutes or until the filling is just set. Refrigerate until
the filling is firm. Sprinkle the top of the tart with sugar.
Place under a hot grill (broiler) until the sugar is golden
and caramelised. Allow the tart to stand for 2 minutes
before cutting into wedges and serving with clotted cream.
Serves 6 to 8.

quince with star anise
on sticky rice

4 quinces, peeled, cored and halved
½ cup sugar
6 star anise
1 vanilla bean*
sticky rice
2 cups black glutinous rice■
4 cups (32 fl oz) water
1 cup (8 fl oz) coconut cream
2 tablespoons palm* or brown sugar

Place the quinces in a saucepan with enough simmering
water to cover them. Add the sugar, star anise and vanilla
bean. Cover the pan and allow to simmer for 2 hours or
until the quinces are soft and have turned pink.
Soak the rice overnight in cold water. Drain and place the
rice in a saucepan with 4 cups (32 fl oz) of water. Cover
and cook over low heat for 10 minutes or until the water
has been absorbed. Add the coconut cream to the rice and
cook over low heat, stirring, until the rice is cooked
through. Stir the palm sugar through the rice. Spoon the
mixture into bowls. Top each with a quince half and a little
of the quince syrup. Serves 6 to 8.
■ See page 34. Available from Asian food stores.

quince with star anise on sticky rice

milk & cream

custard tarts

lemon yoghurt cake

blueberry buttermilk pancakes

little bread and butter puddings

custard tarts

1 quantity or 250g (8 oz) sweet shortcrust pastry*
filling
1 cup (8 fl oz) milk
1 cup (8 fl oz) cream (single or pouring)
1 vanilla bean*
6 eggs
4 tablespoons sugar
freshly grated nutmeg

Preheat the oven to 180°C (350°F). Roll out the pastry on a lightly floured surface until 3mm (⅛ inch) thick. Place in 6 small pie dishes and refrigerate for 30 minutes. Prick the base of the pastry and line with non-stick baking paper. Fill with baking weights or rice. Bake for 5 minutes. Remove the weights and paper and cook for a further 5 minutes.
To make the filling, place the milk, cream and vanilla bean in a saucepan over low heat for 5 minutes. Remove from the heat and allow the milk to stand and cool. Remove the vanilla bean.
Gently whisk the eggs and sugar. Add the milk mixture and combine. Pour the filling into the pastry cases, top with grated nutmeg and bake at 140°C (275°F) for 20 minutes or until the filling is just set. Allow to cool before serving. Serves 6.

blueberry buttermilk pancakes

1 cup self-raising flour*
3 tablespoons caster (superfine) sugar
1 teaspoon bicarbonate of soda (baking soda)
1 egg
45g (1½ oz) butter, melted
1½ cups (12 fl oz) buttermilk
250g (8 oz) blueberries
2 teaspoons grated lemon rind
extra blueberries to serve
honeycomb butter
125g (4 oz) butter, softened
½ cup chopped honeycomb confectionery
1 tablespoon honey

Place the flour, sugar and bicarbonate of soda in a bowl and mix to combine. Place the egg, butter and buttermilk in a separate bowl and whisk to combine. Add the mixture to the flour and sugar. Mix until smooth.
Stir the blueberries and lemon rind through the buttermilk–flour mixture. Pour spoonfuls of mixture into a greased, preheated frying pan over medium heat. Cook for 1 minute each side or until the pancakes are golden.
To make the honeycomb butter, combine the butter, honeycomb and honey.
To serve, place the pancakes in a stack on a serving plate and top the stack with extra blueberries and honeycomb butter. Serves 4.

lemon yoghurt cake

125g (4 oz) butter
1 cup caster (superfine) sugar
2 eggs, lightly beaten
1 cup (8 fl oz) thick plain yoghurt
3 tablespoons lemon juice
1 tablespoon lemon rind
2½ cups self-raising flour*
½ teaspoon bicarbonate of soda (baking soda)
lemon syrup
⅓ cup sugar
½ cup (4 fl oz) water
3 tablespoons lemon juice
rind of 1 lemon, cut in thin strips

Preheat the oven to 180°C (350°F). Place the butter and sugar in a bowl and beat until light and creamy. Add the eggs and beat well.
Stir the yoghurt, lemon juice and rind, flour and bicarbonate of soda into the butter and eggs and mix to combine.
Spoon the mixture into a greased 23cm (9 inch) cake tin. Bake for 45 minutes or until the cake is cooked when tested with a skewer.
To make the syrup, place the sugar, water, lemon juice and lemon rind in a saucepan over low heat. Cook, stirring, until the sugar is dissolved. Allow the syrup to simmer for 4 minutes, then immediately pour over the cake while it is hot and still in the tin. Allow the cake to stand for 5 minutes. Serve with spoonfuls of yoghurt. Serves 10.

little bread and butter butter puddings

2 pears, peeled, cored and sliced
12 small slices panettone or brioche, chopped
4 eggs
1 cup (8 fl oz) cream (single or pouring)
1 cup (8 fl oz) milk
1 teaspoon vanilla extract
2 tablespoons caster (superfine) sugar
brown sugar for sprinkling

Preheat the oven to 180°C (350°F). Grease four 1¼-cup capacity ramekins* or large cappuccino cups with butter. Place the pears and panettone in the ramekins. Combine the eggs, cream, milk, vanilla and sugar. Pour over the panettone and sprinkle with brown sugar. Allow to stand for 5 minutes. Place the ramekins in a baking dish half-filled with water. Place the dish in the oven and cook for 25–30 minutes or until the puddings are firm.
To serve, place the ramekins on a plate or invert the puddings onto a plate and serve with small ramekins of toffee ice cream. Serves 4.

glossary

angel hair pasta
A very thin, tubular pasta – hence its name. Substitutes include spaghetti, linguini, thin fettuccine.

bamboo steamer
An Asian bamboo container with a lid and a slatted base. Placed on top of a saucepan of boiling water, the bamboo steamer holds the foods to be steamed. A metal steamer can also be used. Available from Asian food stores and most kitchen shops.

banana leaves
Leaves of the banana plant, used to wrap food to be cooked. Available from Asian food stores.

basic bun mix
2 tablespoons sugar
1½ cups (12 fl oz) warm water
1 tablespoon dry yeast
5 cups plain (all-purpose) flour
2 tablespoons melted butter or lard

Place the sugar and water in a bowl and stir to dissolve. Add the yeast and leave in a warm place for 5 minutes or until mixture is foamy. Add the flour and melted butter or lard and mix until combined. Place the dough on a lightly floured surface and knead for 4 minutes or until smooth. Roll the dough into a sausage shape and cover with a cloth. Use within 2–3 hours. Makes 1 quantity.

basil oil
Oil that has been infused with basil leaves. Available from good delicatessens.

blanching
A cooking method in which foods are plunged into boiling water for a few seconds, removed from the water and refreshed under cold water, which stops the cooking process. Used to heighten colour and flavour, to firm flesh and to loosen skins.

bocconcini
Fresh Italian mozzarella balls sold in a water or brine solution. Available from delicatessens and supermarkets.

bok choy
A mildly flavoured green also known as Chinese chard or Chinese white cabbage. Limit the cooking time so that it stays green and slightly crisp.

bonito flakes
Shaved flakes of a dried bonito fish. A basic flavouring in Japanese cuisine. Available from Asian food stores.

Calvados
Dry, apple-flavoured brandy, which is named after a town in the Normandy region of France. Substitute apple cider, brandy or sweet cooking wine.

char-grilling
A method of cooking that uses a ridged or slotted hot grill (broiler) either over a barbecue, on an electric char grill, in a char grill pan or on a flat char grill plate that sits on a cooktop. This gives foods a distinct lined pattern and a smoky grilled flavour.

chilli oil
Oil infused with the heat and flavour of chillies. It often has a red tinge.

Different brands have different strengths. Available from Asian food stores and delicatessens.

Chinese barbecue duck
Spiced and glazed duck. Available from Chinese barbecue shops. If necessary, substitute a home-roasted duck.

Chinese barbecue pork
Spiced and glazed pork fillets. Available from Chinese barbecue shops. If necessary, substitute home-roasted pork fillets.

chorizo sausage
A spicy Spanish sausage containing a mixture of pork, pepper and chillies. Available from some butchers and delicatessens.

choy sum
Asian green with small yellow flowers. Also known as Chinese flowering cabbage. Steam or stir-fry the green leaves and tender stems.

coconut vinegar
A cloudy vinegar made from fermented coconut juice. It is usually only 4–6 per cent acidic, which is much lower than other commercially available vinegars. Available from Asian food stores.

crème fraîche
A mixture of sour cream and fresh cream. Substitute sour cream.

curry leaves
Aromatic leaves used fresh or dry to flavour Indian and Southeast Asian dishes. Available from Asian grocers and some supermarkets.

demerara sugar
A dark sugar with hard, dry crystals. The colour comes from molasses. Substitute dark brown sugar if necessary.

dry salted olives
Wrinkled black olives. Available from good delicatessens or grocers.

enoki mushrooms
Also known as enokitake mushrooms. Thin, long-stemmed mushrooms with a mild flavour. Available from good fruit and vegetable shops.

fish sauce
Clear, amber-tinted liquid that is drained from salted, fermented fish. A very important flavouring in Thai cuisine. Available from supermarkets and Asian food stores.

gai larn
Also known as Chinese broccoli or Chinese kale. A leafy vegetable with dark green leaves and small white flowers. The stout stems can be steamed, braised, boiled or stir-fried.

galangal
A root that looks similar to ginger and has a pink tinge. Can be purchased fresh, or sliced and bottled in brine.

green curry paste
A hot and spicy paste of ground green chillies, herbs and spices. Available in bottles from supermarkets or Asian food stores.

haloumi
Firm white cheese made from sheep's milk. It has a stringy texture and is usually sold in brine. Available from delicatessens and some supermarkets.

harissa
A hot paste of red chillies, garlic and olive oil. Available in tubes or jars from delicatessens.

hoisin sauce
A thick, sweet-tasting Chinese sauce made from fermented soy beans, sugar, salt and red rice. Use as a dipping sauce or glaze. Available from Asian food stores and supermarkets.

jap pumpkin
A very sweet and soft variety of pumpkin with a distinctive green and white striped skin.

kaffir lime
A variety of lime with a knobbly outer skin. The fragrant leaves are crushed or shredded and used in cooking, and the limes are used for their juice, mainly in Thai cuisine. Available as packets of leaves or as limes from Asian grocers.

kombu
Japanese kelp seaweed available in dried wide ribbons from Asian food stores.

lemon grass
A tall, lemon-scented grass used in Asian, mainly Thai, cooking. Peel away outer leaves and use the tender root end of the grass. Chop finely or use in pieces to infuse flavour and remove from dish before serving. Available from Asian food stores and good fruit and vegetable shops.

mirin
Heavily sweetened rice wine used as cooking wine. Substitute sweet white wine if unavailable.

miso
A thick paste made from fermented and processed soy beans. Red miso is a combination of barley and soy beans, and yellow miso is a combination of rice and soy beans.

nori sheets
Dried seaweed pressed into square sheets. Use for nori rolls, soups and Japanese cuisine. Keep dry and store in an airtight container. Available in packets from Asian food stores.

oyster mushrooms
Thin-ridged, delicately flavoured, cultivated mushrooms with a slight taste of oysters. Available from good fruit and vegetable shops.

palm sugar
Sap of a palm concentrated into a heavy, moist sugar. Sold in block form and should be grated or shaved before using. Used mainly in Thai cooking. Substitute brown sugar.

pasta

3 cups plain (all-purpose) flour
4 large eggs
2 teaspoons salt

Place the flour on a bench top in a mound. Make a hole in the mound and break the eggs and put the salt into the hole. Break up the eggs with a fork and gradually add flour to the eggs until a rough dough forms. (You can do this step in a food processor.) Place the dough on a lightly floured surface (you may need to add a little water or flour to make the dough manageable) and knead until smooth. Cut the pasta into 4 pieces and roll through a pasta machine or using a rolling pin until it is the desired thickness. Cut the pasta into shapes or cover with a damp cloth if you are using it a few hours later. Cook the pasta in plenty of rapidly boiling salted water until al dente. Make sure the water stays boiling while the pasta cooks. To dry, hang the pasta over a suspended wooden spoon or a clean broom handle for 1–2 hours (depending on the weather), until dry and hard. Store pasta in airtight containers. Makes 1 quantity.

pizza dough

1 teaspoon active dry yeast
pinch sugar
2/3 cup (5 1/2 fl oz) warm water
2 cups plain (all-purpose) flour
1/2 teaspoon salt
1/4 cup (2 fl oz) olive oil

Place the yeast, sugar and water in a bowl and allow to stand until the mixture has bubbles. Add the flour, salt and oil and mix to form a smooth dough. Knead the dough for 5 minutes or until smooth and elastic. Place in a clean, oiled bowl, cover and allow to stand in a warm place for 20 minutes or until it has doubled in size. Makes 1 quantity.

pomegranate molasses

Richly flavoured molasses made from pomegranates, sugar and lemon juice. A traditional product from the eastern Mediterranean. Available from Middle Eastern delicatessens and food stores.

porcini mushrooms

Mushrooms with a meaty texture and a woody, earthy taste. Available fresh in Europe and the United Kingdom, and sold dried in small packets in Australia and the United States of America. Dried porcini should be soaked in hot water before using. Substitute any mushrooms.

ramekins

Small ovenproof dishes used for soufflés and other individually served foods.

red curry paste

A hot and spicy paste of ground red chillies, herbs and spices. Available in bottles from supermarkets or Asian food stores.

rice paper rounds

Also known as rice paper wrappers. Transparent discs made from a ground rice and water paste. Dip into warm water until pliable before using. Available from Asian food stores.

roma tomatoes

Also known as egg tomatoes. Oval-shaped tomatoes, which are great for cooking and eating.

saffron

The dried yellow-orange stigma from the small purple crocus flower (*Crocus sativus*), which is hand cultivated and consequently expensive. Used as a flavouring and colouring. A little goes a long way. Available in both powdered form (which loses its flavour more quickly) and as threads from good supermarkets and delicatessens.

sake

Japanese fermented rice wine. Used in cooking to tenderise and add flavour. Store in a cool dark place and use soon after opening. Substitute dry white wine.

sashimi tuna

Finest quality tuna cut in an Asian or Japanese style. It is very tender and is used raw in Japanese cuisine. Available from good fish markets.

self-raising flour

Also called self-rising flour. To make self-raising flour, simply add 1 teaspoon baking powder to 1 cup plain (all-purpose) flour.

shiitake mushrooms

Originally from Japan and Korea, these mushrooms have a distinctive, full-bodied flavour. They have brownish tops with a creamy underside. Available from good fruit and vegetable stores.

shortcrust pastry

2 cups plain (all-purpose) flour
155g (5 oz) butter, chopped
iced water

Process the flour and butter in a food processor until the mixture has formed fine crumbs. Add enough iced water to form a soft dough. Remove the dough from the food processor and knead lightly. Wrap in plastic wrap and refrigerate for 30 minutes before rolling to prevent shrinkage when baked.
Makes 1 quantity.

sorrel
A hardy perennial herb with a large green leaf belonging to the buckwheat family. Sorrel has a slightly acidic and sour taste due to the presence of oxalic acid. Choose bright green, crisp leaves. Readily available during spring from good fruit and vegetable stores.

sweet shortcrust pastry
2 cups plain (all-purpose) flour
3 tablespoons caster (superfine) sugar
155g (5 oz) butter, chopped
iced water

Place the flour, sugar and butter in a food processor and process until the mixture has formed fine crumbs. Add enough iced water to form a soft dough. Remove the dough from the food processor and knead lightly, wrap in plastic wrap and refrigerate for 30 minutes before rolling to prevent shrinkage when baked.
Makes 1 quantity.

tamarind paste/concentrate
A product from the ripe bean pods of the tamarind tree. It can be purchased as pulp or in the more convenient form of tamarind concentrate ready to use. Used extensively in Asia. Available from Asian food stores.

Thai basil
Includes many varieties such as holy, purple and sweet. Any of these can be used in Thai or Asian cuisines.

Thai pea eggplant
Grown as clusters of small, light green peas. It is bitter in taste and is a traditional ingredient in Thai green curry. Available from Asian food stores.

tortillas
Cornbread baked in flat discs used to wrap foods or eaten as bread. Wheat flour tortillas are another popular variety. Traditionally from Mexico and South American countries. Available from supermarkets.

vanilla bean
Cured pods from the vanilla orchid. Used whole, often split, to infuse flavour into custard or cream-based recipes. Also available is pure vanilla extract, which is a thick, dark, sticky liquid, and makes a good substitute for vanilla beans (use 1 teaspoon for each vanilla bean).

Vietnamese mint
Not a member of the mint family although it is called mint. It has long, green, narrow leaves with purple markings. It is bitter and pungent in flavour. Available from Asian food stores.

wasabi
A spice that comes from a knobbly green root of the Japanese plant *Wasabia japonica*. A traditional condiment served with Japanese sushi and sashimi. It has the same warming or stinging nasal sensation as horseradish. Available in paste or powdered form from Asian grocers.

wonton wrappers
Thin squares or rounds of dough used to enclose fillings when making dumplings in Chinese cuisine. Available fresh or frozen from Asian food stores.

conversion chart

1 cup = 250 ml (8 fl oz)
1 Australian tablespoon = 20 ml
(4 teaspoons)
1 UK tablespoon = 15 ml
(3 teaspoons)
1 teaspoon = 5ml

CUP CONVERSIONS
1 cup almonds, whole = 155g (5 oz)
1 cup breadcrumbs, dried = 125g (4 oz)
1 cup cheese, grated = 125g (4 oz)
1 cup chickpeas = 220g (7 oz)
1 cup coconut, desiccated = 90g (3 oz)
1 cup couscous = 200g (6½ oz)
1 cup flour, white = 125g (4 oz)
1 cup hazlenuts = 170g (5½ oz)
1 cup lentils = 200g (6½ oz)
1 cup mushrooms = 125g (4 oz)
1 cup olives, stoned = 155g (5 oz)
1 cup parsley, chopped = 45g (1½ oz)
1 cup rice, raw = 220g (7 oz)
1 cup sugar, caster = 220g (7 oz)
1 cup sugar, white = 250g (8 oz)
1 cup semolina = 170g (5½ oz)
1 cup watermelon, cubed = 220g (7 oz)

index